Diary of
Reluctant
Green

Diary of a Reluctant Green

Can you save the planet and have a life?

Richard **Hallows**

Editor: Roni Jay

new tricks for old dogs

Published by White Ladder Press Ltd
Great Ambrook, Near Ipplepen, Devon TQ12 5UL
01803 813343
www.whiteladderpress.com

First published in Great Britain in 2007

10 9 8 7 6 5 4 3 2 1

13-digit ISBN 978 1 905410 12 5

British Library Cataloguing in Publication Data
A CIP record for this book can be obtained from the British Library.

Designed and typeset by Julie Martin Ltd
Cover design by Julie Martin Ltd
Cover photograph Jonathon Bosley

Printed and bound by TJ International Ltd, Padstow, Cornwall
Cover printed by St Austell Printing Company
Printed on totally chlorine-free paper
The paper used for the text pages of this book is FSC certified.
FSC (The Forest Stewardship Council) is an international
network to promote responsible management of the world's forests.

FSC
Mixed Sources
Product group from well-managed
forests and other controlled sources

Cert no. SGS-COC-2482
www.fsc.org
© 1996 Forest Stewardship Council

 White Ladder books are distributed in the UK by Virgin Books

White Ladder Press
Great Ambrook, Near Ipplepen, Devon TQ12 5UL
01803 813343
www.whiteladderpress.com

Contents

Preface   5

Introduction   9

Chapter 1   The first 30 days   29

Chapter 2   Month two   76

Chapter 3   Month three   97

Chapter 4   Month four   102

Chapter 5   Month five   108

Chapter 6   Month six   115

Chapter 7   Month seven   125

Chapter 8   Month eight   128

Chapter 9   Month nine   132

Chapter 10   Month ten   136

Chapter 11   Month eleven   139

Chapter 12   Month twelve   143

Chapter 13   Did it do any good?   148

Afterword   161

Appendix   Some hints and tips   163

Footnotes   173

This book is respectfully dedicated to anyone who's ever washed up a yoghurt pot before realising their local authority won't recycle it anyway.

Acknowledgements

A surprisingly large number of people helped with this book by sharing their green experiences and attitudes with me. I would like to thank them all individually, but there are too many to name. I am incredibly grateful for the time and thoughts that they contributed, especially all those who participated in the survey of green issues. I apologise for the difficult questions and for the intense feelings of guilt that the survey seemed to inspire in many who responded, although as one respondent said "Doing this survey was much more fun than working this morning." I hope this book will help to show that however guilty you feel, you are not alone.

I am also extremely grateful to Roni Jay and Richard Craze of White Ladder Press for their support and encouragement.

I must finally thank my wife Debbie, and the kids, Alex and Maria, for tolerating the green experience for the last year. It was more than they either expected or deserved. They have put up with a ban on the clothes dryer, scratchy towels, the absence of pepperoni on a pizza, ecological washing powder, adopted penguins, and the constant shout of 'Can't you turn the bloody lights off'. They have eaten seasonal vegetables (or not eaten them, in the case of a three year old Maria), had showers instead of baths, been denied anything that was over-packaged and even learned what goes in the compost bin and what doesn't. In a statement of ecological solidarity, the kids also regularly failed to flush the toilet.

Preface

"I can answer none of these questions, despite the fact that I consider myself to be very concerned about green issues. Thanks for the wake up call."

Comment from survey respondent, shocked
at their own lack of a green lifestyle.

This is not a book for anyone who is already a committed green activist, unless of course you want to know what being green is like for normal people – who are less green, and more a sort of dark muddy brown. This book is for the vast majority of us who are becoming increasingly worried about some of the green issues that are constantly thrown at us by the media. It's for those of us with an increasing level of eco-guilt, which has yet to translate into eco-activity.

We worry about global warming, but we like to keep the house warm in winter. We worry about the number of miles that food travels before it gets to us, but we can't resist the buy one get one free offer on Kenyan green beans in the supermarket.

We'd like to buy more local food, but too many cheap flights to exotic holiday locations means that we have developed cosmopolitan tastes. Life without olives and sweet potatoes would be a poor one indeed, and anyway the kids wouldn't eat chard and cabbage; at least not more than once. Australian wine is so reliable, and it's always on special offer.

We'd like to buy organic, but the price is ridiculous and the choice so limited. We might even consider organic clothes, but we've never heard of them, don't know where to buy them, and they probably don't do our size. Anyway, none of us has bought a hemp based product since we were teenagers, and that wasn't to wear.

We worry about rising electricity prices, but there's a good reason why we leave the television on standby all the time. We'd like to recycle more, but the council won't collect most of it, and what they do collect they're incredibly picky about. How are we supposed to know what type of plastic they can actually take? We've got better things to do than hang out at the tip (sorry, recycling centre) on a Saturday afternoon, and life's way too short to wash up baked bean tins. If the council didn't want so much rubbish then why did they give us such a big wheelie bin in the first place?

We like the idea of electricity from renewable sources, but those wind farms are destroying the landscape, and it's much more expensive isn't it?

It's a worry. It feels as if all we ever hear about is the impact we are having on the environment.

As we throw another empty wine bottle in the wheelie bin, we can hear the radio discussion concerning the fact that there are no longer any landfill sites available and we will have to export our waste to China.

As we get in the car to drive the 500 yards to the shops we're pretty sure that the polar ice caps will last until we're all dead and buried, except of course there's no room to be buried any more, so we'll have to be cremated, thereby making our final contribution to greenhouse gases.

As we go to bed at night, we are blissfully unaware that there are more than 20 electrical devices still eating electricity in the house while we sleep.

This book will help you do your little bit to save the planet. It will show you why you should do something and what you can do without giving up soap, or dedicating your life to recycling your underwear. It will show you:

1 How you can dramatically reduce the amount of waste you produce

2 How you can save on your electricity bills

3 How you can save money on your shopping bills

The book draws on a survey of many other similar people who are trying to be greener and it will provide you with the strategies and the evidence you need to change your habits so that you can be 'greener' without sacrificing your lifestyle or reducing your standard of living.

It's an epic struggle between 21st century convenience and environmentally responsible behaviour, as one uncommitted family fights to save the planet at least a little bit.

Introduction

As a rule I am completely in favour of the conveniences of modern life. I like to be able to go on holiday to far away places using low cost flights; I cannot imagine life without disposable nappies; I like to be able to buy food that requires little more culinary skill than the ability to set the microwave to the right time, and I like to be able just to throw things in the wheelie bin. Life is much too short to spend time separating the rubbish and washing dirty nappies.

I am not a natural 'green'. My instincts are a sort of muddy brown, although in my particular case, I am not sure that I am making a significant contribution to the destruction of the planet. I haven't cut down a swathe of rainforest the size of Wales, pumped billions of gallons of sewage into the sea, or melted a polar ice cap, but I am now starting to think that my lifestyle is no longer environmentally sustainable.

Like all of us, I am regularly subjected to newspaper reports and television programmes telling me a wide range of often conflicting facts concerning the state of the environment, and the expected apocalyptic results of the damage we are causing to the planet. It is conceivable that I am just easily influenced, but then again, it is also possible that someone might have a point. This is enough to worry me. It seems that it is also enough to worry most people. In the survey conducted for

this book the percentage of people 'concerned' or 'very concerned' about specific issues was:

Environmental Issue	Percentage Concerned or Very Concerned
Destruction of Wildlife	81%
Climate Change and Global Warming	73%
Fair Trade	68%
Water Shortages	63%
Waste and Recycling	59%
Road Traffic Pollution	57%
Use of Pesticides	49%
Energy Security	48%
Food Miles	38%
Air Traffic Pollution	35%

So, somewhat unsurprisingly, it seems that most of us are worried about something to do with the environment. What is less clear is whether 'being concerned' is enough either to prompt us, or to enable us to do anything about it. I have a personal suspicion that the apparent lack of concern about air traffic pollution may well be driven by an even greater concern that we may at some point be forced to stop taking cheap flights to exotic locations in order to drink Margaritas on the beach.

Given that 49% of those surveyed for this book were concerned about the use of pesticides, only 6.3% always bought
organic food. With 68% concerned about fair trade, only
22.2% bought fair trade goods when they were available, and
with 38% concerned about food miles, only 7.9% always
bought locally produced food.

It would be possible to avoid the supermarket and eat only
locally grown produce, or food that we had grown ourselves,
but this would involve eating only seasonally available foods
and returning to a diet that (in the UK at least) was last experienced by a peasant population with a life expectancy of
about 35. This does not sound as if it would be progress, or as
if my kids would put up with it for more than the first meal.
We all expect to be able to eat salad at any time of the year,
and enjoy our pasta, olive oil, bottled water, Australian wine;
the list goes on and on. If you look in the shopping trolley the
next time you do a weekly shop, if your shopping hasn't
clocked up 100,000 miles, you're probably doing well.

There are lots of environmental issues to worry about, and not
that much that can be done about them without a significant
change in lifestyle. My reasons for going green are not just
concern about environmental issues, and I am not planning a
significant lifestyle change. They are reasons of enlightened
self-interest at three levels.

Firstly, our weekly shopping bill is now the size of the national
debt of a small island nation. I am embarrassed to admit
that although I know how much I spend in the supermarket
every week, I would be hard pressed to say exactly what I spent

it on. I am also fairly sure that I throw away about half of what I buy.

Secondly, my electricity bills have grown significantly over the last few years. Once again, I have no idea why we use so much electricity, or what we use it for. I would like to believe that the meter is inaccurate, but I think this is a false hope.

The third reason why I would like to adopt a greener lifestyle is to reduce the amount of rubbish that we produce from our household. Every week there is a full wheelie bin plus additional black bags left outside the gate for the local authority to collect. The ability to dispose of the amount of rubbish we produce is an increasing problem and an increasing cost for local authorities.

It is very easy to throw things away. It is much easier than recycling things, reusing them or doing anything else with them. Anything I throw away doesn't need washing, crushing, or checking to see if it can be put in a recycling basket. It is the easy option. It is also the option that is used for most rubbish in the UK, and most of it ends up in a landfill site somewhere.

In 2003/4 of all the household waste produced 19% was recycled or composted, 9% was incinerated and 72% was sent to a landfill site[1]. By 2005 the recycling rate was up to 23%, and even though this is an improvement, given what I know we throw away, that strikes me as shameful. It probably should be noted that the USA recycles something like 28% of its waste. It feels incredibly embarrassing to discover that we recycle less than the population of the USA, who according to the popular view are the epitome of environmental couldn't care less.

Landfill is particularly bad from an environmental perspective because of what it is we throw away. Organic waste that goes into landfill produces methane gas, which is particularly bad for global warming, and chemicals from land fill sites can seep into the water courses, thus poisoning the natural water supply. This would also fit neatly in the category of 'a bad thing'.

But enlightened self-interest will definitely apply to the issue of sending waste to landfill. There is to be a new penalty for local authorities who exceed a government set landfill allowance. For every additional tonne of waste over and above the allowance that is sent to a landfill site, a local authority will be fined £150. Although I have no supernatural powers that enable me to see the future, I am fairly certain that this will end up on my council tax bill. In Switzerland, for example, recycling is free but throwing anything away as rubbish costs money. Every waste bag has to have a prepaid sticker attached to it or it isn't collected. This is what they now call 'pay as you throw'.

I am fairly sure that most of the waste we produce could be avoided if we were smarter about it. I am hoping that a desire to reduce the amount of waste we produce will provide the incentive to change the way we buy things. Ideally, I expect this to lead to a reduction in the amount of money I have to give to a major supermarket chain every week.

I just do not believe that I am going to save the planet by washing up yoghurt pots or making sure I put the newspaper out for recycling. I doubt whether installing new insulation is going to make a great difference to the future existence of polar bears and penguins either. However, I am still willing to give at least some of it a try.

Sadly, not all of us are leaders of a political party; at the stage of life when we can pack it all in and live in a mud hut; or have the financial wherewithal to buy everything that seems to be needed to go green. I'm sure there's an irony somewhere in the fact that going green seems to be becoming an excuse for more consumption. Green gadgets and technology have become the latest essential accessory, at least among the portion of the population yet to get to grips with camera phones. You could spend a fortune saving the planet by installing insulation, double glazing, solar panels, a domestic wind turbine and a rainwater collection system. You could buy a hybrid or electric car, organic clothes and wind-up radios; the list is almost endless.

Not all of this expenditure would seem to make the slightest sense to me. As an example, there is a cheap domestic wind turbine on the market for about £750. This will produce enough electricity to power three low energy light bulbs, or about 60 watts per hour. Domestic electricity currently costs somewhere in the order of 10 pence per kilowatt hour. This means that installing a wind turbine will save me somewhere in the region of 0.6 pence per hour. Assuming I have three lights on continuously, this means that it will be 125,000 hours, or 5,208 days, or 14 years, before this wind turbine saves any money. Given that the lights are on for less than a quarter of the day this is probably closer to 56 years before this saves anything at all. This sounds like a bizarre waste of money to me, and given the fact that there must be some environmental cost in the manufacture and distribution of a domestic wind turbine, I would doubt if it is particularly environmentally friendly to install one anyway. It may be that my natural disinclination to invest in anything that only pays back at a point in time when I no longer expect to be here is probably a microcosm of the whole problem with making any kind of sacrifice to save the planet. Of course I realise I should be thinking of future generations, so I have asked my five year old if he would like me to put a wind turbine on the house, but he says he would rather have a Power Ranger.

This is an example of what seems to me to be one of the biggest problems with trying to go green.

1 It's probably a complete waste of time anyway. Why turn the taps off when there are three leaks in the main within five miles of where I live?

2 Getting out of bed in the morning has an environmental cost associated with it. Anything you do has some kind of environmental cost. The thought of carrying round some sort of eco-guilt all day every day is probably only going to make the manufacturers of antidepressants smile.

3 There are almost always trade offs to be made in any environmental analysis of a situation. Dishwasher or handwashing? The dishwasher uses less water but uses electricity. Use

an old power hungry appliance or replace it with a new energy efficient one? The energy efficient one uses less electricity but there are all the costs of its production and distribution to be considered. The correct environmental choice is not as obvious as it might be.

4 There is insufficient information available for people to be able to make an environmental choice at the point of consumption. If I checked all the packaging on what I buy in the supermarket to see if it could be recycled, I would be there for a week. And the labelling on electrical goods seems to be an absolute disgrace for the most part, as it gives no idea of the environmental impact that new games console is going to have.

5 As well as insufficient information there are massive amounts of conflicting information as well. Real nappies or disposables? Real nappies don't end up in landfill, but there is the environmental cost of cleaning them. We all know packaging is bad, or is it? If there was no packaging then how much food would be damaged in transport and thrown away? Suddenly nuclear power stations are greener than an organic cabbage which, it turns out, isn't green at all because it was flown in from somewhere you would have to look up in an atlas.

6 But most of the information, as well as insufficient and conflicting, seems to be fundamentally unreliable. Nobody really seems to have any definitive answers about anything.

It was the amount of conflicting and untrustworthy information that prompted me to do a survey specifically for this book, in an attempt to try and gather first hand, subjective views of how people are responding to the anticipated environmental apocalypse that lies before us. It's not a hugely scientific survey, but it does focus on what the issues are that prevent us all from leading a greener lifestyle.

One thing that came out of the survey was that it wasn't out of a lack of will. In many cases it was out of a lack of perceived opportunity. Almost a quarter of all the responses to the survey were accompanied by an apology for their environmental misdemeanours. I suspect this shows that if the huge amount of media coverage has done nothing else, it has at least succeeded in adding a massive additional weight to the burden of middle class guilt.

However, although we're all feeling incredibly guilty about environmental issues, this is combined with a fairly significant lack of awareness of both the problems, and the potential solutions.

As part of the survey, a number of questions were included in order to see how people perceived some of the green issues. Even allowing for a margin of error of plus or minus 50%[2] the number of people whose perception was incorrect is astounding given the volume of media coverage of green issues, and the amount of money spent by government agencies to try and get the environmental message across.

- 87% did not know how many tonnes of household waste is sent to landfill each year (21.9 tonnes per household)

- 90% did not know what the proposed fine per tonne would be for excess landfill (£150 per tonne)

- 81% did not know how many litres of water would be used by leaving the tap on while brushing their teeth (30 litres)

- 77% had no idea how much water is used per person per day in the UK (155 litres)

Interestingly there was some variation in whether perceptions were better or worse than reality. There were two areas where perception was worse than reality:

- 51% estimated the UK recycling' rate to be worse than it really is

- 58% thought that more household waste went to landfill than is actually the case

However, in most areas the survey suggested that people believe the situation to be better than it really is. For example 70% thought that more of the UK's electricity supply comes from renewables than is actually the case, and 79% thought that the water use per person was less than the 155 litres per day we use.

So, despite the fact that it seems as if everyone is worried about environmental issues, we still seem to have a perception that things are better than they really are, and that our ability to impact the environment is less than it really is. This is pretty much a fairly good summary of how I feel about things as well.

One other area shown by the survey was that people took the environmentally friendly option when it was easy; for example, with doorstep recycling collection. Where the potential to recycle easily was not provided, most took the easy option and threw stuff in the trash.

For the most part though we seem to be a fairly positive bunch about what impact we can have. In the survey for this book 90% felt that if the UK was greener it would make a difference to global warming and 55% felt that by recycling whatever could be recycled we could reduce the amount of household waste sent to landfill by between 40% and 70%. However, more than half of all respondents (51%) felt that a greener lifestyle would also be more expensive. This isn't a huge surprise to me. If anything I am more surprised that 49% of people felt that being greener would cost about the same or even be cheaper. I am hoping to prove the 49% right and show that it is possible to be greener and save some money at the same time.

Before I started to think about what would be involved in being greener in our daily life, I honestly thought we weren't too bad. Unfortunately this seems to be a remarkably good example of the self-delusion that all of us seem to inflict upon ourselves when we think about how environmentally friendly we are. Sadly, the acts of buying one or two energy efficient light bulbs and giving old baby clothes to a relative are not enough.

Unfortunately, even where I thought we were good, it seems there may be more complexities at work than I am aware of.

For example, all of our double glazing is UPVC, which seemed like a good idea at the time. However, the production of UPVC is generally thought to be hugely damaging to the environment. This is the first of many ironies. Our electric showers probably aren't saving us any money at all. The hot water is already available in the immersion heater, and we are using electricity to heat cold water to have a shower. Our thermostatic valves on the radiators are only going to control the temperature in a room rather than do anything to stop the central heating from running. So, even when I thought we had environmentally positive attributes, these again may have been merely an act of self-delusion.

All in all I think we're a relatively normal family. We're worried about the environment, and about what's happening around us, but probably not worried enough to do anything about it that would cost us money. We don't buy organic food, we leave the television on standby just so we don't have to get up from the couch to turn it on, when we've already got the remote control in our hands. I don't think we're particularly bad about our approach to the environment, but I'm certain we're not particularly good, and I suspect we should try to do better. There, that's enthusiasm for you!

However, it should be said that there are no really good ways to measure how green a family is. In an attempt to try and measure how much damage we do to the environment, I have discovered the twilight world of the carbon footprint calculators. This is a very scary place indeed. They are relatively simple (and free) services on the internet that enable anyone to input their mileage, flights, home details, electricity bills, eating habits and the like, and it will then take these parameters and use them to calculate the amount of carbon dioxide you are emitting into the atmosphere, and so give some indication of how much environmental impact your existence has on the planet. I have a suspicion that this may be something of an inexact science, but it is all that's available, and it is free.

There seem to be as many carbon footprint or environmental impact calculators as there are websites claiming to be able to help you to do something about it. The results are somewhat varied. For example:

- British Petroleum (**www.bp.com**) thinks my household is emitting 24 tonnes of CO_2 per annum, as opposed to a UK average of 9.85 tonnes. This doesn't sound good at all

- Carbon Footprint (**www.carbonfootprint.com**) tells me that I am emitting 36,825 kg per year for me as an individual as opposed to a UK average of 10,963 for an individual. This sounds even worse

- CO_2 Balance.Com (**www.co2balance.com**) tells me that I am emitting 46.25 tonnes of CO2 for the household per annum, for which I apparently need to plant 43 trees

- Earthday (**www.earthday.net**) suggests it would need 9.3 hectares to support my lifestyle, or 5.2 planets if everyone lived like me

I have to be honest in that I am pretty disappointed with all of these results. To discover I am consuming 5.2 planets is something of a shock. In order to reduce this feeling of shock I redo all the carbon footprint calculators but lie outrageously about my lifestyle. Somehow the results don't improve that much. I feel as if I have been strip mining sites of special scientific interest and dumping the waste in areas of outstanding natural beauty, when in fact I had thought I was just living a relatively normal life. My eco-guilt level has gone off the scale.

However, call me cynical if you like, but it is an uncanny coincidence that the lowest carbon footprint value is produced by the website of a global oil company, and the highest value by an organisation that also provides the opportunity for me to give them money to plant trees on my behalf. Funny that, don't you think?

There is also some difficulty in my mind as to what it really means to be green. There seem to be as many ways to be green as there are green pressure groups concerned about a particular environmental issue. There also seems to be a trend towards being more than just green, but being ethical as well. Unfortunately, I suspect that ethical living is likely to be beyond my comprehension let alone my capacity for change.

A quick evaluation of the green landscape suggests that I am going to have to set some limits. Depending on what you read, going green seems to include everything from becoming a vegetarian through riding a bicycle and eating organic, to using solar and wind power. There is no way that I or my family are going to achieve this environmental nirvana, but presumably any effort to reduce our impact on the environment is better than continuing as we are.

Part of the problem with trying to be greener is that even before I've started, it feels as if I could get stuck in some intellectual mud of trying to figure out whether what I am doing is actually greener than the alternatives, or in fact what the environmental impacts of my actions are at all.

Without giving it all up in order to live in a 'dwelling made from natural material' (mud hut to you and me) the number of things to consider in order to try and be green is absolutely mind boggling. In summary it could be described as being aware of the environmental impact of everything you do, and doing whatever you can to minimise it. So, for example, a relatively minor purchase of, let's say, a new mobile phone, would probably need the following things to be taken into account:

1 The environmental impact of mobile phone masts

2 The environmental impact of cables and microwave systems used to connect the mast to the telephone network

3 The manufacturing process involved in creating mobile phone masts, fibre optic cables and microwave systems

4 The environmental costs of the manufacture of the telephone

5 Where it was manufactured and using what kind of labour

6 The environmental impact of the electricity required to charge the phone, and whether a solar powered charger should be purchased

7 The impact of radio waves used in the telephone's operation

8 The environmental impact of the transport and distribution of the telephone

9 How the telephone is to be disposed of when finished with

10 How much of the telephone can be reused or recycled

11 How much recycled material was used in the original manufacture

12 The amount of packaging used for the telephone

And if I was prepared to sit here long enough I could think of another 50 environmental issues that I should consider every time I not only buy a new telephone, but every time I pick one up to use it. I haven't even mentioned disruption to marine life from undersea telephone cables, or debris in space from obsolete satellites. I could go on (and on and on and on).

This is the kind of thinking that just makes me want to say forget it (or something like that) and not even bother taking the most basic environmental issues into account in my day to day life. I could probably drive myself into a state of almost total inactivity if I worried about every possible aspect that seems to be considered green in some way. It is clear that some boundaries are required.

The first boundary is that I am going to concern myself only with being environmentally friendly, rather than with being 'ethical'. As an aside, the whole concept of being ethical seems somewhat dubious, as it means that a judgement of right or wrong needs to be made concerning almost any action. I don't think ethical is going to work for me as I don't have the time or the emotional capacity for guilt to evaluate the ethical dimension of every minor decision I make; it is very unlikely that I have all the information available to me that would be required to make an accurate ethical decision; and what I consider to be ethical may be different from the people who have decided to sell me a product with a label that states that it is ethical.

I am expecting that there is going to be a cost associated with being more environmentally friendly. I don't think anyone makes environmentally harmful products just to ensure they are more expensive. They make them because they are not forced to pay for the environmental damage that their production incurs. The environmental damage is therefore a cost that is hidden, both for the consumer and the producer. As there will almost inevitably be a direct cost incurred in producing goods in a more environmentally friendly way, I expect that more environmentally friendly food and goods will be more expensive. Due to the unfortunate fact that I have yet to win the lottery, cost is a consideration. Incredible as it may sound, I am prepared to pay something of a premium in order to be greener; just not that much of a premium. The second limitation I shall put on greenness is that it should not carry an increased cost of more than 5%. Even within these parameters I expect there to be a lot that I can do in order to reduce my personal damaging impact on the environment, and in particular, the current doomsday scenarios surrounding climate change.

There are some contributing factors to climate change that I can do nothing about. For example, cows. There are 1.4 billion cows in the world that produce 500 litres of methane a day – each. That is 14% of the total methane emission in the world. Methane has 23 times the global warming potential of carbon dioxide, so this is, strange as it may sound, an important issue for climate change[3]. Perhaps I'll try and reduce the cow population by eating more beef.

But it gets worse. There are the trees to consider. It seems that trees, while reducing the effects of carbon dioxide emissions, also produce methane. Trees may account for anywhere between 10% and 30% of the global methane pumped into the atmosphere[4]. The irony of the fact that we consider planting more trees to be good for the environment, when they may be producing a far more harmful greenhouse gas, just goes to show how complicated any consideration of our impact on the environment can be.

Unfortunately my science education stopped when I was 16 so it is difficult for me to make any significant contribution to the debate on the science of climate change. Fortunately there are a lot of people who seem to be quite prepared to make their opinions known. As far as I can make out, nobody seems to be denying that there is some climate change currently in progress, but there is disagreement about whether this is mainly a result of human activity, and whether it will lead to the catastrophic results that are so fondly enjoyed by special effects editors in film and television.

We are frequently told that we have 10 years or so in which to bring our carbon emissions under control or we will permanently damage planet earth. Of course, for everyone who tells you there are 10 years left to save the planet, there's someone who will tell you it's already too late; and there's someone who will argue that it doesn't matter anyway, because there are unimagined technological advances that will undoubtedly solve all the climate problems we predict for the future. There are even a few who will argue that even if it isn't too late, and even if we could save the planet by changing our way of life, we really shouldn't because it would be a direct contravention of God's will. Personally I was planning to do everything I could to postpone the apocalypse for as long as possible. There are also those who will argue that climate change and global warming are merely the products of over active imaginations.

Evidence from the International Panel on Climate Change in Climate Change 2001 shows that there is definitely something happening, as shown by increases in the average surface temperature, decreases in snow and ice cover, decreases in ice thickness, the retreat of mountain glaciers, rises in average sea levels and increases in the atmospheric concentration of carbon dioxide.

An alternative theory is that large scale climate change is caused by the amount of solar energy reaching the earth rather than any concentration of greenhouse gases. The levels of solar energy being determined by:

- The shape of the Earth's orbit which varies on a 100,000 year cycle.

- The tilt of the Earth's axis which varies on a cycle every 41,000 years.

- The precession of the equinoxes on a cycle of every 22,000 years.[5]

While I admit to not really understanding a word of the above, it did sound very convincing to me. Of course, then it is reported that the George C Marshall Institute that presented these findings is in part funded by the oil industry[6]. No wonder I'm confused. There is always the possibility that it's a conspiracy between the cows and the trees to destroy the planet and all human life along with it[7].

I am not going to worry unduly about the rights or wrongs of the reasons for going green. I am comfortable with the idea that I may well save money, feel healthier, and be prepared for the day when the riot squad are automatically deployed in response to the microchip in the lid detecting an errant banana skin being placed in the wrong wheelie bin. The amount of information available and the sheer complexity of weighing up every single issue for every single decision is enough to make me want to stop before I have started. I can't worry whether fair trade goods are being unfairly marked up by the supermarkets, or whether some fair trade countries still use child labour, or even what the environmental costs are of the production of plastic toys in far off lands. It just makes everything too hard.

CHAPTER 1

The first 30 days

"My husband has started putting one cup of water in the kettle. Every time I go to make a quick cup of tea there's no water in there. It's bloody annoying."

DAY ONE

I am gripped with enthusiasm on my first day of being green. I have visited a number of websites belonging to green organisations that are full of blinding glimpses of the obvious to help the newly converted.

My first action is to sign up for the mail preference service. This has the effect of telling all direct mail marketing companies that they can no longer send direct mail to your home. About 70% of the mail we receive is unsolicited direct mail. I suspect that I will miss the emotional boost that comes from knowing that I have been pre-approved to receive huge sums of money at outrageous rates of interest, but this is one sacrifice I am prepared to make.

The Mailing Preference Service

The Mailing Preference Service (MPS) is one of a set of preference services that are free to subscribe to and prevent unsolicited marketing material from reaching you. There is also the Telephone Preference Service (TPS), Fax Preference Service (FPS) and the Baby Preference Service (which cuts down mailings of baby-related products and services). The easiest way to register is online at **www.mpsonline.org.uk**, although it is also possible to register by telephone on 0845 7034599.

They claim that registration will reduce direct mail by 95%.[8]

DAY TWO

In line with advice from various websites I have turned down the thermostat that controls our central heating. Most of these sites suggest turning it down by one degree. In a continuing burst of enthusiasm I have turned ours down by three degrees. Less than an hour after doing this my wife walks into the room. The conversation went something like:

"Is there something wrong with the heating?"
"I don't think so."
"It's freezing in here."

At that point she turned the thermostat back up to a point somewhere beyond where it had been in the first place. So much for that idea. Secretly I turn it back down later in the day – but not as far. She doesn't notice.

DAY THREE

As one of the most common pieces of advice I have seen about how to save electricity is to switch things off rather than to leave them on standby, I have decided to try and break what can only be described as a standby dependency. This is proving somewhat difficult as the couch is very nearly a whole seven feet away from the television. The remote control is only six inches from my fingertips.

Ironically, the standby dependency is not as much of a problem when turning off the television as it is when turning it back on again. I don't mind getting up from the couch and making a short diversion via the off button. The problem is that I don't like falling into the seat and reaching for the remote control only to realise I haven't turned the television on, which means I have to get up again. Now I wouldn't say I was lazy, but this is proving a heavy burden to carry.

It's not just the television either. Standby is a problem with the CD player as well, which stays on standby unless it's been switched off at the wall. This has always struck me as a particularly stupid design feature. The computer monitor is almost always left as a blank screen on standby as well.

I have, fortunately, discovered an easy answer to the television problem, which is to get my three year old to go and switch the television on for me. She thinks this is great fun as she isn't allowed to touch the television. I'm not sure what you do if you haven't got a three year old though.

I know that standby alone isn't going to fix our electricity problem. Most days we are using over 40 kilowatt/hours. A kilowatt is a thousand watts, so a kilowatt hour is the equivalent of leaving ten 100 watt light bulbs on for an hour, so our daily usage is close to leaving 20 100 watt bulbs on for 24 hours a day. Even by my standards this seems ridiculous.

At the moment it is a bit of a case of trial and error in terms of trying to discover how all this electricity is being used, but there is no harm in switching things off if we're not actually using them. I'm surprised at just how much can actually be switched off. In particular there are two power tools in the garage that are left on almost permanent charge, and I am using an old laptop computer that stays plugged in overnight. Switching these off seems to have an almost immediate effect on the speed with which the power company is able to take my money away. Some further analysis of the situation shows that the battery on the laptop has actually given up the ghost. (I don't use it on battery power so I have never noticed before.) As a result, the battery isn't holding any charge, so all the time it was switched on it was pulling power trying to charge a battery that was never going to be fully charged. This, as an aside, has also explained why the office used to get so warm all the time.

Battery chargers seem to be particularly bad for electricity consumption, probably because of our tendency to leave them switched on for long periods of time, even when they no longer need to be charging. Apparently, if we all switched off mobile phone chargers overnight this would save enough electricity to power 66,000 homes for a year, and would have the added benefit of reducing how much time we all spend making meaningless telephone calls.

DAY FOUR

One of the areas of life that we clearly have to improve in order to be greener is our use of the car. In some ways we have already (admittedly by accident) improved the way in which we use the car in that I work at home for five days a week, while my wife also works from home at least two days a week. Although this means we have increased electricity usage from the regular coffee intake required to get through the day, and the inevitable computers, printers, and massaging chairs that no good home office could be without, it does mean our commuting cost to the environment is a lot less than it has been in the past. (The massaging chair is just wishful thinking by the way.)

Road traffic pollution and congestion is probably the single environmental issue I notice more than anything else. Over the last few years my annual mileage has been about 8,500 miles per annum, even though I rarely have to drive long distances any more, and the fact that driving into London was a deeply distressing experience has always discouraged me far more than any congestion charge ever could. (If anything, a reduced traffic load in London makes driving there seem more attractive.) I only have to drive round the North Circular or even make it onto the M25 to be convinced of the need to do something about the amount of time all of us seem to spend in the car.

I'm sure everyone has a reasonable excuse for why they're using the car. After all, there's no public transport system to speak of, travelling by rail into London is one of the few things that can make the M25 seem like a pleasant experience, the days when the kids could be thrown out of the house on their bike and told to go to school on their own seem to be long gone in many cases, and if you want to go shopping it's a long walk to the out of town malls and retail parks.

Of course, my family has good excuses as well.

We live rurally and are six miles from the nearest shop. The village shop and post office closed down in the nineteen seventies, and the pub soon followed. Both are now desirable village homes called 'The Old Post Office' and 'The Old Red Lion' respectively. Our nearest pub is now four miles away.

There is no public transport at all. Sorry, there is a bus that goes past the end of the road to the nearest town on a Tuesday morning. The return bus comes back on a Thursday. Of course the strange thing is that they seem surprised that nobody uses it.

The kids go to school and preschool six miles away. (This was our catchment area school I hasten to add, so this isn't a parental choice to drive them miles past the nearest school in order for them to be taught by nuns.) We could send them on the school bus, but the bus stop's three miles away so it hardly seems worth it. Anyway, even in my greenest moments the idea of putting a five year old and a three year old on the bus isn't going to fly. There is always the option of home schooling

I suppose. The five year old is quite attracted by this idea as he suspects it will involve a lot of time watching television. I am less attracted to the idea as I suspect it would involve a complete nervous breakdown on my part somewhere in the first term.

We are not going to eliminate our use of the car as part of being greener, so the main things that we can do as a family are to:

- Reduce our car mileage by eliminating unnecessary journeys

- Use the greener car option by avoiding the use of the 4x4 unless absolutely necessary

- Combine journeys so that, for example, instead of picking up the kids, dropping them off and then going to do the shopping (total journey 24 miles) I would pick up the kids and then do the shopping with them (oh joy) before returning home (total journey 14 miles)

This sounds great in theory. It is also probably the best that I can expect to do. I am not going to cycle 12 miles a day with a trailer full of kids behind me, and selling the car and replacing it with something more environmentally friendly strikes me as a futile gesture until the point at which the car really needs replacing.

DAY FIVE

I am already turning into the light police, switching lights off when there is nobody in the room. I am thinking about imposing a room sharing policy on the household, so that lights may only be used if there is more than one person in the room. On reflection, this may be excessive, but I am convinced that we have the potential to be a lot more environmentally friendly in the way we use electricity. From a distance, the house frequently resembles Blackpool Illuminations, and I understand that pilots of night flights into Heathrow and Luton use it as a marker to ensure they are on the correct approach. The main sounds in the house (if you tune out the screaming children) are the sounds of the dishwasher, the washing machine and the dryer. I don't think we're significantly different from most other family homes, but I can see where we could potentially reduce our electricity usage. If this has the added effect of helping me to reduce the amount of money I have to give to Powergen on a quarterly basis, then that would be a bonus.

In an attempt to set a baseline I have been trying to find out how much electricity the average household uses. According to Powergen this is 14 kilowatts per day – so the equivalent of having about six 100 watt light bulbs on for 24 hours a day. At first sight this doesn't seem unreasonable if it wasn't for the fact that we are currently using more than 40 kilowatt hours per day. I wondered whether someone had typed 14 when they meant 40 as the average usage, but it seems they really did mean 14. After an analysis of our previous quarterly bill it seems that we used 36 kilowatts per day. I suspect this is an error due to an estimated reading from the meter, but after tracking back over the last 12 months our average electricity usage is now 38 kilowatts per day. I am shocked. This is more than two and a half times the national average, and is also costing me nearly £300 a quarter. Desperate measures are called for. I hang up some washing to dry rather than put it in the dryer and feel immediately better despite the fact I will probably have nothing to wear tomorrow.

DAY SIX

Despite my success with the laptop computer, I remain confused about where all this electricity is being used, so I have decided to track the meter reading throughout the day. More washing has been hung out to dry. The whole of the downstairs of the house resembles a very badly organised laundry service and the dining room carpet has been stained by a dripping red sock.

Looking at some of the advice available, the basics for saving electricity without spending anything in order to save it are:

- Switch off things when they aren't needed rather than leaving them on standby

- Turn the heating thermostat down by 1°C. Done that but without much success

- For cooking, use the right size pan and cut the food into smaller pieces and put lids on pans. This will make the food cook a lot more quickly

- Use the microwave for heating things up and defrosting as this is more efficient than a conventional oven

- Regularly defrost your freezer and keep it packed full, even if this is with scrunched up paper to avoid wasting energy

- Only wash full loads and use a lower temperature setting on the washing machine. This can save up to 75% of the cost when compared with using the hottest cycles

- Only fill the kettle with the water that is needed [9]

None of these ideas seem particularly useful, or likely to reduce our electricity usage by twenty two kilowatt hours a day. More thought is clearly required.

As it is shopping day, one thing I have decided to do is to try and avoid using plastic bags. I have spent part of the day searching through the cupboards to find the reusable shopping bags that I know we have got somewhere. I depart for the shopping trip armed with three canvas bags that were given to me on business trips some years ago and a large bag that we acquired from a French supermarket where they no longer issue you with plastic bags at the checkout. I am not sure what I am going to do for bin liners in the kitchen bin now, but the 20,000 plastic bags we have stored around the house will probably help.

Estimates vary, but some suggest that every year somewhere around 18 billion (yes, that's billion) plastic bags are given away in the UK. That's more than 300 for every man, woman and child in the UK. I haven't kept count, but given that I go to the supermarket every week and it results in at least 10 plastic bags, I have been responsible for more than 500 of them. I thought I was being clever by using them as bin liners, but it seems that nearly 80% of us do the same, so it's not that clever after all. I suppose it's a form of reuse, but it still ends up in landfill.

For me, using plastic bags has always just been a matter of convenience. I always thought it was easier to use the plastic bags rather than have my own reusable bags. I am not too proud to admit that I was wrong.

I am not sure what determines the size of a plastic bag. Presumably it is a complex formula determined by the size and weight of what is being sold and the strength of the plastic. Or it could just be that they are exactly the right size to be used as a small bin liner. The reusable bags are generally much larger. This has the surprising side effect of making shopping much easier. The 10 plastic bags have been reduced to five reusable bags. This means that it is quicker to pack, quicker to get the bags from trolley to car, quicker to get them from the car to the house, and quicker to unpack them at the other end. Bizarrely, switching to reusable bags has actually improved the shopping experience. They are easier to use, more convenient, and environmentally friendly. It might sound like a small thing, but I am incredibly pleased about this.

As well as making the shopping easier I am also reducing my carbon emissions. It is estimated that shoppers who use throwaway plastic bags create 25.14 kilograms of carbon dioxide per annum, whereas cotton reusable bag users are producing only 0.62 kilograms per annum[10]. Sadly, I suspect this isn't enough to cover flying to the USA on holiday, but it's a start.

Plastic bags are also an environmental hazard, particularly for marine life. According to the Marine Conservation Society large numbers of them end up on UK beaches. In a 2004 beach survey 39 bags were found for every kilometer of beach surveyed. Plastic bags can be mistaken for food and have been found in the stomachs of many marine animals including endangered species such as leatherback turtles, harbour porpoises and black footed albatross and have also been recorded as a cause of entanglement of marine animals[11]. So for the 81% of the survey who were concerned about the destruction of wildlife, refusing to use disposable plastic bags is one way to turn that concern into action.

DAY SEVEN

The first results of a detailed look at the electricity usage are now in. Bizarrely our usage overnight is 14 kilowatts. We are consuming the average amount of electricity for a normal household while we are asleep. Clearly, something is seriously wrong.

An inventory of the electrical appliances switched on overnight is surprising.

1 Fridges (x 2)
2 Freezers (x 2)
3 Telephone handsets (x 4)

4 Mobile telephones on charge (x 2)

5 Radio alarm clocks (x 2)

6 CD players (x 2)

7 ADSL router and print server in the office

8 Night lights (x 3)

9 Home security system

10 Telephone/Fax machine

11 Septic tank pump

12 TV signal booster

13 Mains wired smoke alarms (x 2)

14 Baby monitor (transmitter and receiver units)

15 Freeview box on standby

16 Sky digibox on standby

17 TV on standby

18 DVD on standby

19 VCR on standby

20 Mains wired outside light timer

At a rough estimate there are 33 electrical devices that are consuming power to some degree while we are asleep. Immediately, I unplug the radio alarm clock in the guest bedroom although I doubt this was the main culprit. The next obvious step is to turn some of these devices off rather than leave them on standby all the time.

DAY EIGHT

The dramatic steps taken to reduce electricity usage overnight do not seem to have made any significant difference. As the office is lit up like a Christmas Tree, I have decided that will be the next area to attack. This necessitates the rearrangement of the plugs so that anything that can be switched off at night is on a single switch, making it easy to switch off in the evening and on again in the morning. One thing that has become clear very early on is that if there is a significant amount of real effort involved in reducing consumption then it is just not going to happen, so making it easy to switch things off is essential.

Where I can't organise things sufficiently in a wall socket I have purchased strip plugs where each individual socket has its own switch. This will enable anything that doesn't need to be powered overnight to be effectively switched off at the wall. The experience with the laptop has left me somewhat paranoid about devices that use electricity when I think they're off.

DAY NINE

Overnight electricity usage has gone down from 14 kilowatts to 11. The 24 hour usage has reduced from 40 something kilowatts to 32. While there is still obviously room for improvement, and I am at a complete loss to understand how anybody can live while using only fourteen kilowatts a day unless they live in the dark and eat out a lot, this is a lot better than it was. Perhaps the most depressing thing about this initial review of our power usage is that it wasn't a case of overusing electricity it was a case of just plain wasting it. We weren't even 'using' the electricity we were consuming as most of the time we were asleep. In less than a week we have reduced our electricity consumption by 30%. I fully intend to write to the government and let them know they should put these new nuclear power plants on hold for a while. Now it's just a question of keeping that up and not getting back into bad habits and also looking at where normal usage can be reduced.

DAY TEN

It is another ecologically momentous day for me today. Not only did I remember to take my reusable shopping bags to the supermarket, and not only did I manage to keep the shopping bill down below 75% of what it used to be, I have also bought my first environmentally friendly product. I have taken the first step towards becoming an eco-shopper. Admittedly the purchase of a bottle of Ecover washing up liquid (with Chamomile and Marigold) is a very small step to becoming a fully fledged eco-shopper, but "one small step for a man" and all that.

I am confidently expecting it to be complete rubbish and to be back on the environmentally less friendly usual brand of washing up liquid within a week. My logic for this low expectation is that

i   Nobody would actively do anything as part of their manufacturing process to damage the environment if they didn't have to

ii Therefore anyone who claims to be specifically not damaging the environment in their manufacturing process must be omitting some essential part of the process iii Therefore their product will not work as well as the product that does not claim to be good for the environment

iv Any product that is good for the environment will also be more expensive

The first shock is that it is no more expensive than the chemical concoction I normally buy. The second shock is that I don't understand anything that is written on the label. This includes in the ingredients list:

"15% plant based anionic and non-ionic tension-active surfactants"

Is that English? I consider myself to be basically literate but I don't even recognise the words, let alone the sentence. Ecover seems to be a Belgian company. It is possible that this is English written by a Belgian without an adequate review process. It is also possible, like so much in the green arena, that it has been written by people who just don't seem to get out enough. The whole green subculture seems to have invented its own language and underlying principles that exclude the rest of us from doing anything other than separating our trash while those more knowledgeable can berate us for not being aware of what our carbon footprint is. It strikes me that the green industry has got to find a way of communicating with the rest of us that:

1 Uses words we can understand. (This would seem to be a basic requirement of all communication, but one that the green community has apparently overlooked)

2 Doesn't talk down to us

3 Talks in terms we can relate to. (It's all very well telling me how many tonnes of carbon monoxide I produce every year, but frankly that doesn't mean a thing to me)

4 Provides us with the information that allows us to do something to change, rather than just makes us feel guilty about it

5 Stops criticising people for being unable to make changes that are impossible to make. There is no bus that comes within three miles of my house more than once a week, it is six miles to the nearest shop, and I have two kids under the age of five. I will not be giving up my car any time soon.

The rest of the Ecover label is a fabulous example of what can be done when you combine bad writing with ecological doublespeak.

Although I have managed to eke out the remains of my usual brand of washing up liquid until dinner time, the bottle is now empty and the first use of Ecover is imminent. The bottle promises it "cleans effectively without producing excessive bubbles," so I am on the look out for anemic bubbles that don't clean effectively, but I am completely distracted by the smell. I assume this is the chamomile and marigold although I couldn't tell you which, but the smell is amazing. Suddenly this is just part washing up and part aromatherapy. The smell is strangely soporific, and I can feel myself becoming more and more relaxed as the washing up progresses. This is not what I normally feel when I am doing the washing up. The sink is empty far too soon, and I spend the next 20 minutes looking for more things to wash up. For a moment I seriously consider bathing the kids in it as well. If being environmentally friendly can make washing up an enjoyable experience then I am all for it. The dinner plates don't look too bad either, but at this point that has become a secondary consideration.

After the success of the Ecover washing up liquid, a quick scan of the shelves in our local supermarket showed no other environmentally friendly products alongside all the rest of the brightly coloured chemicals. More importantly there seem to be no more products that smell of camomile and marigold. A search of their website (**www.ecover.com**) shows a huge range of cleaning products. If they all smell as good as the washing up liquid then I will have the cleanest home in Britain. Sadly I can find nowhere to buy them. Once again from the Ecover website:

"Do you want to know where you can buy Ecover in your country? Please get in contact with our local distributor. Good Luck."

There is something about the fact that they end the sentence by wishing us good luck in tracking down their products that leads me to believe it may not be as easy as one would hope. I have sent an email to the supermarket head office instead asking them why they don't stock more than just the washing up liquid. I await their response with interest.

DAY 11

Some further research has started to give some indication of where the electricity is going.

i   A fridge uses between 1 and 1.5 kilowatt hours per day

ii A freezer uses about 1 kilowatt hour per day

iii A dishwasher cycle uses about 1.5 kilowatt hours

In our house, these three things account for 6.5 kilowatt hours per day of the 25 we are still using. Just the remaining 25.5 kilowatt hours to figure out now then.

DAY 12

I have started to look more seriously at what we recycle. Our recycling efforts have always been somewhat sporadic, and as our local authority collects the recycling once a fortnight and I can't be bothered to crush cans or squash plastic bottles, and they provide baskets just about big enough for one day's worth of recycling, most of it ends in the wheelie bin. As I think it's unlikely that my desire to spend my days not crushing cans is likely to change I have made a quick trip to the local council offices where they have happily sold me three more recycling baskets at £1 each which I do not begrudge them. Now everything that can be recycled will be recycled, at least as far as the plastic, paper and cans that the local authority will collect.

Annoyingly, our local council doesn't do a doorstep collection of anything other than plastic, newspaper and tin cans. Things such as bottles, clothes, shoes, cardboard and green waste that are collected by some other local authorities still need to be taken to the tip (sorry, recycling centre). Even with the best will in the world, it is unlikely that I am going to make it there on a regular basis, and it is even more unlikely that I am going to go there with a week's worth of rotting vegetables in the car. I am becoming resigned to the fact that the garage is soon going to be full of old clothes, shoes, cardboard boxes and bottles waiting to be taken for recycling. Where they will go among the old tins of paint, bits of wood, broken furniture and half finished do-it-yourself projects is a mystery. It is a long time since our garage saw a car.

DAY 13

As the biggest part of my regular miles is the school run at the moment, in order to try and minimise the miles I do, I have been experimenting with the route. It seems that I had sub-consciously decided on the route with the least number of junctions in it, which is a mile longer than the obvious alternative route. This would be 10 miles a week. Or over the year 390 miles just in the daily school run, plus the numerous other occasions I seem to be at the school for some reason or other. This doesn't sound a lot, but as it now looks as if I will only do something in the order of 4–5,000 miles in the year, this is nearly 10% of my total mileage. I am pleasantly surprised that I can save 10% of my annual mileage by adding three left turns to the journey.

According to **co2balance.com** this is equivalent to 75 kilograms of carbon dioxide and would require me to plant one tree to offset it. This would cost about £8. The petrol for 390 miles would currently cost me about £60. Considering that most of the cost of that is tax, it strikes me that there is probably scope for the government to take the hit and offset all the carbon emissions out of their fuel tax revenues. I shall write to the Chancellor who I confidently expect will ignore my suggestion that he should use tax money to offset my carbon emissions.

DAY 14

As one of the main reasons why I want to adopt a greener lifestyle is to reduce the amount of waste we send to landfill I have (and this sounds much more sad than it really is) had a look at the waste that we actually produce. There are some significant contributions.

1 Disposable nappies. If I could have a young child who didn't need nappies I would have, but in the meantime, at least 20% of our waste is disposable nappies.

2 Cat litter. Two kittens that have both just had the op and so are not allowed outside at the moment are producing a bag of used cat litter every day. This is about 10% of our waste. There are many reasons why I am looking forward to the day when they can once again enjoy the great outdoors.

3 Organic Matter. While we don't put grass cuttings or the like in our rubbish, there is a lot of kitchen waste that could be composted rather than thrown out. This is about 10% of our rubbish.

4 Glass makes up about 20% of the weekly wheelie bin. This is a combination of wine bottles and glass food jars. OK, not that many food jars. The local authority does not currently collect glass from our house. There are a number of areas that were deemed too difficult to access for the glass collection vehicle. It is a six mile drive to the nearest glass bottle dump, which is in the supermarket car park. Somewhat stupidly (it seems to me) the bottle dump is on the exit route from the car park rather than the entry route. It would make far more sense to me if I could take the bottles, dump them (and so empty the boot of the car) and then do the shopping that will fit neatly in the now empty boot of the car. Somehow, the positioning of the bottle dump on the exit is stopping me from wanting to recycle glass. I freely admit this is a pathetic reason for not bothering to recycle glass, but there it is.

5 Cardboard of some sort or other also makes up a huge amount of the weekly waste, by volume if not by weight. The sheer number of waste cardboard items produced every week by our household is a shock. On a perfectly average week:

- 2 cereal boxes

- 3 toilet roll tubes (these are often reused for making model rocket ships or telescopes, but eventually they have to be thrown out)

- 2 kitchen roll tubes

- 1 flapjack box

- 1 cereal bar box

- 1 rice box

- 1 tea bag box

- 4 tissue boxes (we've all got colds)

- 1 coffee filter paper box

- 1 egg box

- 1 washing powder box

- 3 medicine boxes (that were used to package another container with the medicine in it)

- 3 tetrapak cartons for orange juice

- 7 unidentifiable boxes that seemed to belong to toys

Everything seems to be in a cardboard box. Even if it is packaged in a plastic bottle, the plastic bottle seems to come in a cardboard box. For some reason I had never noticed this before. Cardboard is also not something that is collected for recycling. Much of this seems as if it would not be something that could be recycled anyway, for example the tetrapak cartons have a plastic lining, and the tissue boxes include some plastic to guide the tissues out. I would estimate that another 20% of the wheelie bin is taken up by cardboard.

The remaining 20% is a mishmash of occasional items that are thrown out including steel cans, waste food, electrical items, clothes, shoes, and the like.

By a quite bizarre and fortuitous coincidence we have, today, been left a plastic box with a letter telling us that the local authority will now be collecting glass as well as newspaper, plastic and tins, but only once a month. My first thought is that this is great news. My second thought is that the box clearly isn't big enough for the amount of glass waste that we produce in a month. This is a worry as it probably means I'm drinking too much – or at least more than the council thinks I should be drinking. Still, at least it's a start.

Looking for answers to the problem of waste is a difficult one as there is a lot of it that it seems impossible to do anything about. If they don't sell the stuff in packaging that can be recycled then what can I as the consumer do about it? About the only recourse I have is to refrain from buying the stuff that is overpackaged or packaged in non-recyclable packaging, despite the fact that this would describe most of our weekly shopping purchases.

However, some answers are available:

1 Cat litter. The cats are going to learn where outside is and quick. The only reason why we're using cat litter is because they have both just had the op and so aren't allowed out for a few weeks.

2 Kitchen waste. We are going to get a compost bin for the garden, and make beautiful, rich compost that we shall then use to fertilise our own kitchen garden. A vision of a green idyll appears before me.

3 Cardboard. This is going to be used for kindling over the winter when we have wood fires while the family sits round

listening to the wireless and toasting tea cakes on long forks. (OK, the idyllic vision is getting a bit much.) What we will do with cardboard in the summer remains a conundrum.

4 Glass. We now have the glass collection service, so that should not be a big problem. It is also an incentive to be better about recycling overall. I promise myself that I will now wash up cans and put them out with the plastic.

5 Disposable nappies. No thoughts on that one as yet. I have my limits.

DAY 15

It is a day I never thought I would live to see. Today I washed up a yoghurt pot so that it could go in the recycling. I am feeling inordinately proud of myself and convinced that this simple effort will undoubtedly stave off the collapse of the ice caps for many years.

At the same time as washing up the yoghurt pot I also rinsed out a baked bean tin as our local authority will also collect aluminium and steel cans for recycling. This is a good thing as every tonne of steel cans recycled saves 1.5 tonnes of iron ore and 0.5 tonnes of coal and the use of scrap steel uses 75% less energy than is needed to make steel from new materials. The only sad thing about this is that of the 13 billion steel cans made every year only about 2 billion are recycled. [12]

A number of the remaining 11 billion are in what I call my

'Year 2K millennium bug, the world's going to end and guess who will be eating tinned grapefruit for the next 30 years' storage shed, but most of the 11 billion will be going into landfill, which is crazy, especially when steel is apparently one of the easiest materials to recycle.

I have to admit that the main reason why I have never bothered recycling food tins before is that I always imagined they would be difficult to wash up. This is not the case. Most tins wash up more easily than the plates, and rinse out in the old washing up water without any problem at all. This is a very pleasant surprise. There are of course all the risks associated with handling sharpened steel, but at the moment I still have all my fingers.

DAY 16

An environmental tragedy has occurred in this small corner of our green and pleasant land. On a quarterly basis the local council sends out a regular newsletter to all its council tax paying citizens (with what we pay it should really be gold embossed and hand delivered by liveried staff, but that's another story). In this particular issue there is a fascinating article on recycling. The particularly interesting part of it is that not all plastic can be included in the recycling collection baskets – even if it has the recycling logo embossed in the plastic.

Worse still, they specifically mention yoghurt pots. It seems that the inclusion of just one yoghurt pot in a truck load of plastic destined for recycling will result in the whole consignment being rejected by the recycling plant and sent to landfill instead. Fortunately it only takes me 20 minutes to extract all the yoghurt pots from the recycling baskets and put them in the rubbish instead, which is annoying as they have all been washed.

It seems that the recycling logo may be completely worthless as an indication of what is practically possible for the normal person. It appears that having the recycling logo on some packaging really means that this packaging could be theoretically recycled, if someone invented a means of recycling it and then built a whole new recycling plant in order to be able to do it. I may be becoming cynical, but it is starting to seem as if where you see the words 'recyclable where facilities exist' what they actually mean is that 'there is no way you could ever recycle this in a million years.'

Meanwhile, back in the real world, the only plastics that can be included in our recycling collection are those that have the number 1, 2, or 3 in the middle of the recycling logo. This would specifically exclude all the yoghurt pots that have a 6. They don't make it easy do they?

Plastics Recycling

There is a whole range of plastics that can be identified by the logo that should be printed on the plastic packaging or product. The type of plastic determines whether a particular item can be recycled or not, or whether it results in several tons of plastic being dumped into landfill.

Product or packaging made from Polythene Terepthalate, whatever that may be. Most plastic drinks bottles are made of this.

Product or packaging made from High Density Polythene. This can be represented as PEHD on some packaging, and includes bleach bottles and other household cleaning materials.

Product or packaging made from PVC. I had some clothes made of PVC once, but the less said about that the better.

Product or packaging made from low density Polythene. This includes the kind of packaging you would typically find on strawberries in a supermarket.

Product or packaging made from Polypropylene.

Product or packaging made from Polystyrene. This includes yoghurt pots. I am not sure whether to be more worried about the fact that I can't recycle them, or that I am eating something out of polystyrene.

Product or packaging made of something else plasticky.[13]

Now that I know that even if something looks like plastic and feels like plastic, it can't necessarily be defined as plastic for the purposes of recycling I have started to look a little more closely at the plastic packaging we acquire to see if it really is recyclable.

The first shock is just how much packaging isn't even marked to say what it is. It doesn't even rate the all encompassing 'other' definition. The second shock is that there is a large number of things that are outside the 1,2 and 3 that the local authority is prepared to collect.

As an example, in the house at the moment there are the following items in plastic packaging that are OK.

- Fizzy drinks – PET (1)
- Plastic pill bottles – HDPE (2)
- Cleaning supplies – HDPE (2)
- Bubble bath (for the kids you understand) – HDPE (2)
- Shampoo – HDPE (2)
- Mouthwash – PET (1)
- Milk – marked PEHD, which is just a confusing way of marking it HDPE (2)

Unrecyclable plastic items include:

- Toothpaste pump dispenser – unmarked
- Margarine tub – unmarked
- Coleslaw tub – unmarked
- Humous tub – unmarked
- Yoghurt pots – PS (06)
- Ketchup bottle – PP (05)
- Cream cheese container – PP (05)
- Make up remover bottle – PP (05)

While I admit that it was unlikely that I was ever going to wash up the empty ketchup bottle, it is disappointing that however hard I try, it looks as if a fair amount of plastic is going to end up in the wheelie bin regardless. As I said, they don't make it easy. Just to make it even more difficult, the packaging is almost always marked on the bottom. My suggestion, having just mopped up two pints of milk from the kitchen floor is either to:

a Make sure the lid is on properly before checking what the packaging is made of

b Check it once it's empty, or

c Check it in the supermarket before bringing it home

Option c is by far the best thing to do, as if the top isn't on, someone who works for the supermarket will have to clean up the mess, you won't have already paid for it, and most importantly you still have the chance to try and find a replacement product that is in recyclable packaging.

DAY 17

It is shopping day again. Following my near disaster with the yoghurt pots I have come to what may seem to be an obvious conclusion, but has taken me this long to reach. It is now clear to me that as far as managing household waste and recycling goes, by the time I am standing in the kitchen looking at an empty container it is actually too late for me to really do anything about it. In order to manage what waste and recycling goes out of the house I have got to be more conscientious about managing what comes into the house. I have to be more careful about what I buy. This will include:

1 Trying to stick to the shopping list, which is difficult with a small child who randomly grabs anything close to hand and adds it to the shopping cart

2 Avoiding anything that has a lot of packaging

3 Buying loose fruit and vegetables rather than prepackaged

4 Ensuring that where products do have packaging, that it is something that can be recycled

In an attempt to avoid packaging that I can't recycle, I have switched the family from orange juice (available only in tetra-pak cartons) to a Tropical Fruit Drink that comes in a PEHD plastic recyclable bottle. This has a 2 in the middle of the recycling logo. I think I'm getting the hang of this.

DAY 18

It is a day for reflection, having managed to reduce the shopping bill by 30% yesterday, but with a significant amount of money still having been spent on disposable nappies. Apparently I am going to spend nearly £1,000 on disposable nappies in the first two and a half years of my daughter's life[14]. I am well aware of the fact that I could probably achieve a reduction in household waste and a reduction in the weekly shopping bill by switching to reusable nappies. So why don't I?

There is something about being able to fold up a dirty nappy and just put it in a plastic bag and never have to think of it again that seems to outweigh any environmental cost. I have spent the last five years changing nappies[15] and even with the convenience of disposables that is what I would refer to as 'a big ask'. The idea of changing to something that I perceive as less convenient, and harder work, at a point where I can just about see the potential for potty training the youngest child is frankly horrific. I have absolutely no intention of using reusable nappies. In order to reduce the amount of waste we put into the system I will make sacrifices in other areas. I have resolved to make the cats go outside in the garden with immediate effect. I will also get my youngest child potty trained in record time.

The great nappy debate is an interesting one. I have seen first hand the emotion that it can create, and I have to tell you that the inclination not to open this particular bag of worms (so to speak) is a strong one. However, I do not wish to be considered a coward, so here's a quick summary of the debate.

1 Reusable nappies good, disposable nappies bad

2 Reusable nappies need more resources to wash them than disposables consume

There, that's about it. Not enough? Then read on.

Nearly three billion nappies are thrown away every year in the UK, and 90% of these make their way into landfill. This represents between 2% and 3% of all household waste, or some 400,000 tonnes[16]. That's a lot of nappies by anybody's standards.

Reusable nappies have come a long way from the huge terry cloth sheets and oversized safety pins that were a part of my (somewhat distant) childhood. There is a dazzling array of styles and systems that can be used, both if you want to wash nappies at home, or if you want to use a nappy laundry service to wash them for you. You can check out **www. snazzypants.co.uk**, **www.eco-babes.co.uk**, **www.nappymania.co.uk**, **www.happyheinys.co.uk** (my personal favourite internet domain name of all time by the way) if you need more details.

The main part of the argument is that by using reusable nappies the environmental impact is reduced by:

- Not sending disposable nappies to landfill or for incineration

- Not using finite resources in the production of nappies that are then thrown away

What seems to be the most comprehensive UK research into nappy use (right down to details on average urine and faeces volumes, which is way more than I ever wanted to know) seems to be from the Environment Agency in a report published in May 2005. This research concluded that there was no significant difference in the environmental impact of all three possible nappy systems (home washing reusable, laundry service reusable and disposables).

As you can imagine if you had been washing nappies for the last several years in order to save the planet, this was something of a disappointment to a lot of people. As a result, the findings of the Environment Agency are disputed, and it is claimed that it is possible to reduce the environmental impact of real nappy use by 24% against that found by the Environment Agency[17].

Some of the more esoteric costs of disposable nappies were also omitted from the calculations, for example, the costs to Thames Water of the 8,000 annual instances of blocked pipes caused by the flushing of disposable nappies down the toilet[18].

I would dearly love for my daughter to be able to wear my green credentials by using reusable nappies, but I just cannot get past the convenience and ease of use of a system that involves buying a disposable nappy from a supermarket, using it and then disposing of it by putting it in the rubbish. I know this is awful, but this is one area where I think the costs and the inconvenience (and additional effort) of moving to reusable nappies is not something I am prepared to take on. I do, however, vow to potty train my daughter at the earliest possible convenience.

There is of course the alternative of an environmentally friendly disposable nappy. There are now nappies and nappy sacks that are claimed to be biodegradable. (There's not much point putting a biodegradable nappy inside a non-biodegradable nappy sack.) However, as always, nothing can be completely simple. There are elements of the biodegradable nappies that are better for the environment in that they tend to be unbleached and they contain less of the cocktail of chemicals that are in a normal disposable nappy. However, they need to be composted in order to biodegrade effectively, as landfill lacks the environment required to help them breakdown. As far as waste disposal goes, buying biodegradable nappies and putting them into the wheelie bin isn't much better than buying a normal one.

The most effective way of composting biodegradable nappies seems to be by using a wormery to break them down, however, nobody that I can find will guarantee that this will remove all the pathogens that could be contained in a full nappy. I am afraid the idea of a wormery in the garden full of old nappies really does not appeal.

DAY 19

As I now seem to be locked in a running battle with the house one room at a time, I have decided to get smarter with the dishwasher. It has become a habit to run the dishwasher every night before going to bed, so that in the morning there are clean dishes for breakfast and hopefully everything is dry and can be taken out and put away with the minimum of effort. The dishwasher gets run every evening whether it really needs it or not. At a guess I would say that it is normally about two thirds full. This means that if I ran it only when it was full I should be able to reduce the number of times it is run by about a third. Over a year, this would be a reduction of something in the order of 120 times. Considering a dishwasher uses 1.5 kilowatt hours of electricity, this would save 180 kilowatt hours in a year. If I owned shares in an electricity company I would sell them now.

Disappointingly the first time of doing this means that the

plates from a very pleasant tortellini with tomato and mozzarella sauce have been sitting in the dishwasher for 20 hours and did not get clean, so I have left them in to be run again. The answer is to change the water heat setting on the dishwasher to 65 degrees centigrade rather than the 50 degrees we had been running it on. I have the horrible suspicion that any saving I have made has just been completely wiped out. However, getting smarter with the dishwasher and the washing machine will save water as well as electricity.

DAY 20

My joy at reducing our tetrapak consumption to zero has been completely destroyed by the information that the tropical fruit drink I have bought as a replacement for orange juice is in fact packed with additional sugar and who knows what else. Because it is called tropical fruit *drink* rather than tropical fruit *juice* it is apparently acceptable for it to have almost no natural ingredients, little nutritional value, and enough added sugar to keep the kids going all day and probably all night as well.

Sneaky huh? What I don't understand is why orange juice (the healthy option) has to be sold in non-recyclable cartons (oops, sorry, recyclable where facilities exist) and tropical fruit drink (the less healthy sugar enhanced option) is sold in a carton that is fully recyclable. I am afraid if it is a choice between pumping the kids full of sugar or being unable to recycle the carton, I will have to continue putting the tetrapak cartons in the wheelie bin.[19] I have enough trouble with the kids being hyper without adding even more sugar to their diet.

However, I have also now made my second eco-purchase, and have bought half a dozen environmentally friendly light bulbs which only use 11 watts to give a 60 watt equivalent light. These are very strange things that also have some strange characteristics. The ones I have can't be used with lights that have a passive infrared sensor (movement sensor) on them, and they can't be used with dimmer switches. Fortunately we don't have any dimmer switches in the house so this isn't going to be a problem.

They take a bit of getting used to though. They take a second or so to switch on and they give a light that doesn't seem to be as bright as our normal 60 watt bulbs. In some of the rooms in the house I give up as they just aren't going to make the room bright enough, but where I can live with a dull half light and in some cases a strange buzzing noise from the light socket, I have installed these power saving light bulbs. They are expensive to buy, but with a 15 year expected life, they make sense, even though I am not naturally predisposed to buy light bulbs that may be here longer than me.

DAY 21

The same local authority magazine that alerted me to the issues involved in the unauthorised inclusion of yoghurt pots in a recycling basket also includes details of the availability of subsidised composting bins from the local authority. As part of our waste minimisation plan, and given that a lot of our waste seems to be vegetable kitchen waste that could be composted, I have ordered two of them to go in the garden.

Many local authorities will provide heavily subsidised home composting equipment. In this case it seems they have subsidised more than 80% of the cost of buying a compost bin from the local hardware store, which I have to say is very nice of them (unless you own the local hardware store).

DAY 22

The composting bins have arrived and have been installed in the garden. As they are both empty at the moment, they are both being blown around the garden by the wind. Hopefully this will not happen once we start to put rotting vegetable matter inside them. I had imagined that composting would be an easy activity but it seems that, once again, being green is somewhat more complicated than I could have possibly imagined.

Firstly, there are a number of things that should not go into a composting bin, including:

- Cat litter
- Cooked vegetables
- Meat
- Milk and dairy products
- Nappies
- Perennial garden weeds and weeds with seed heads (i.e. most of the weeds in my garden)
- Used tissues

Items that can be put in a composting bin include:

- Vegetable peelings
- Citrus fruit peelings (although these take longer to break down)
- Grass cuttings
- Cardboard
- Egg shells
- Newspaper can be added as scrunched up sheets to aid aeration
- Plant prunings
- Tea bags and coffee grounds

The important thing (it seems) is to get a good mix of greens (grass, vegetable peelings and the like) and browns such as cardboard, tea bags, and other woody items, to add fibre. This composting bin seems to need a more balanced diet than the children which is a worry.

One of the things I am looking forward to with a composting bin is that, just like any other interesting hobby, there are lots of accessories that I can get. This is what I am sure will make me a serious professional composter. The sieve for lumpy compost, the aerating tool, the compost breaking down fluid for grass, and the caddy for kitchen waste have all suddenly become potential future birthday gifts from family members.

The issue of getting kitchen waste from the kitchen to the composting bin is one that has obviously exercised better minds than mine at some stage, and so there is a range of caddies that can be used. I have an old bin that I fill up until it is either full or my wife complains about the smell. I can tell that this is going to be a problem. The task of carrying this bin across the garden to the compost bin and then washing it out is going to get annoying.

DAY 23

The good news at this stage is that the waste reduction plan for the household seems to be working. Now there are four full recycling baskets out waiting for collection and the wheelie bin is only half full rather than overflowing. This is a genuine surprise to me that such a huge difference has been made just by:

1 Trying to buy things that aren't over packaged

2 Recycling whatever we can that gets collected by the local authority

3 Not putting cardboard out in the rubbish

4 Composting the kitchen waste

5 Getting the cats to go outside

Admittedly the garage is full of cardboard boxes, but I'm sure I'll find a use for them some time soon. However, even with disposable nappies, we now have a less than half full wheelie bin. This is probably a 60% reduction in our overall waste going to landfill which, however imperfect it may be, is still pretty amazing I think.

DAY 26

It is taking some time to get used to the idea of composting. My first instinct is to throw things into the kitchen bin rather than to save it for the composting bin. I am also finding that the compost bin being at the other end of the garden from the house might be the best place in terms of the smell I am expecting it to create, but it is certainly not the most convenient place for it to be if I am ever going to use it. I am continuing to leave mounds of rotting vegetable peelings lying around the kitchen, which has the advantage of making the cat's behaviour more interesting than usual, but is also annoying my wife.

DAY 27

I have had to swap some of the long life light bulbs I had installed, as living in a dull half-light wasn't practical in some areas of the house. They are definitely an acquired taste.

DAY 28

I believe I may have discovered the biggest waste of energy in existence – telling a five year old to turn the lights off when he leaves the room. In an attempt to make this more amusing (at least for me) I have taken to using my best Michael Caine impression and adapting a line from *The Italian Job*, telling him "You're only supposed to turn the bloody lights off." He doesn't seem to find this particularly funny, but I have today had a complaint from a parent that they discovered their own child walking round the house telling everyone to "turn the bloody lights off." When asked where they got such language they ratted out my son without an apparent second thought.

DAY 29

I have continued to monitor electricity usage on a daily basis. The daily consumption has now reduced from more than 40 kilowatt hours to 28. However, today there was a spike in consumption. This seems to have been due to doing the ironing. This seems to be another significant benefit of going green; a reasonable excuse for not doing the ironing.

An unscientific and fairly random test of the use of other electrical appliances now shows that the vacuum cleaner is also a major contributor to greenhouse gases. I resolve to stop vacuuming and ironing with immediate effect.

As well as looking at how much electricity we use, I have also tried to have a good look at when we use it in order to try and work out how best to avoid such excessive consumption. The graph below shows the way in which we use electricity over the day by showing how much we use in an hour as a percentage of the total daily use.

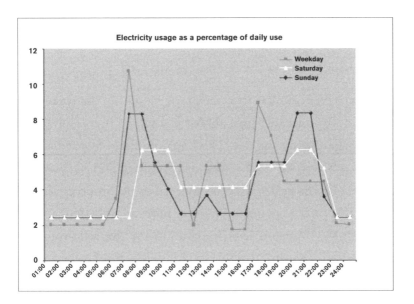

There are several areas that seem interesting. Firstly, there are three very different profiles depending on whether it is a weekday, a Saturday or a Sunday.

A weekday tends to have an extended spike in usage between six and nine in the morning. This isn't vastly surprising as it is a result of everyone showering, making cups of tea and coffee, and making toast, as well as lights going on while the curtains are still drawn or it is dark outside.

Weekday usage then tails off to a relatively stable rate while we are working, with a small spike at lunchtime. However, as the kids come home from school, we cook dinner, and inevitably end up watching television, using the computer, and switching lights on, so the usage climbs in the evening. It then spikes again as we go into the late evening which seems to be a result of things being switched on in the evening and then not turned off until bedtime, so as the evening goes on there is more and more being used, until it is switched off and there is then a sudden fall in the amount being used.

Saturday is very similar to a weekday except that the spikes are much more dramatic, probably as a result of there being less work usage during the day. The morning usage is particularly high as this is when the house gets vacuumed and the washing goes on. The Saturday evening usage is a lower percentage of the total Saturday usage and tails off more rapidly than a week day mainly as there is less preparation for the following day required on a Saturday night, so computers tend to be off.

Sundays are different again in that the usage is much more even across the day. This is probably a result of the whole family being at home and the fact that everything is a bit more relaxed on a Sunday without such a hectic round of washing and vacuuming.

This has helped to give a little bit of focus to where some actions should be taken in order to reduce some of the electricity usage.

- We should make sure we switch things off when they're not being used in the evening rather than waiting until going to bed

- We need to look at the overnight usage which is still something over 2% of the daily use per hour, which means that overnight is about 16% of our total use

Of course, we could stop showering or cleaning the house as well.

DAY 30

I have over the last month been thinking about the way we do the washing. As with a lot of green activity, this sounds sadder than it really is by the way. I have cut out using the dryer, which means the whole house smells of damp clothes, and we now have towels with both the drying properties and the texture of coarse sandpaper, but nobody said that going green wouldn't mean the occasional sacrifice. The children are unhappy about the towels.

We also seem to have somehow got into the habit of wearing clothes once between washes. A quick inspection of the washing pile (which is always there because I have to wait for the last load to dry before I can wash any more) suggests that just over 80% of the washing is already clean. This strikes me as not only a waste of energy but also a waste of my time.

Resolution number one is not to wash clean clothes any more. This is a shame because we have only just trained the children to put clothes in the washing basket when they take them off rather than leave them spread around the floor. We have also switched the washing machine to run on a cold cycle. This should reduce its use of hot water, and so reduce the amount of time the boiler runs to heat the water for other uses. Changing the washing machine onto cold doesn't seem to result in any significant difference in what the clothes look like when they come out. This isn't too surprising as most of them were already clean when they went in.

Unfortunately things aren't going quite so well with the dishwasher. My resolution to run it only when full is continuing unchanged, but unfortunately we continue to have the problem of dirty plates sitting in the dishwasher longer before being washed. It is giving the breakfast cereal a greater opportunity to set on the plate like cement. I'm fairly sure that if I ran the dishwasher long enough I would destroy all the plates and be left with just a very clean blob of hard Weetabix. I am naturally disinclined to start washing things a second time by hand, and most things seem to have been fixed by the increased temperature at which the dishwasher runs. The only answer is to rinse some of the dishes before putting them in the dishwasher, even though this is not a good use of water.

The good news is that at least in terms of water usage, running the dishwasher seems to be generally considered as more environmentally friendly than hand washing the dishes. This is an immense relief as I had been wondering what the carbon emissions were from the manufacturing process involved in a pair of rubber gloves and whether I could use that to justify the dishwasher.

All in all, the first month feels as if it has been a success.

- The rubbish is significantly reduced

- Our home composting environment is running smoothly, if a little smelly at times

- We aren't using standby as much on the electrical appliances

- We've unplugged a lot of electrical items that we weren't using, but which were costing us money even when we weren't using them

- I have a good excuse for skipping on vacuuming and ironing

On the down side, I am still exercised by the huge electrical usage in the house which I need to try and get to the bottom of. I definitely feel greener. Well, maybe less brown.

CHAPTER 2

Month two

After the excitement of the first month during which I have increased our volume of recycling by a factor of five, and reduced our contribution to the landfill of the English countryside by something like 60%, it all seems to have come to something of a standstill. Our recycling is now fairly significant at a basic level.

1 Clothes are recycled either by:

    a Being given to a charity shop

    b Being given to relatives (in the case of baby clothes)

    c Being left at the clothes bank in the local car park, including shoes

    d A remarkable transformation into a dust rag

2 Newspapers and magazines are collected by the local authority recycling scheme

3 Glass is collected by the local authority recycling scheme

4 Aluminium cans are collected by the local authority recycling scheme

5 Steel cans are collected by the local authority recycling scheme

6 Plastic is collected by the local authority recycling scheme (as long as it is PET, HDPE, or PVC)

7 Books and toys are given to friends or charity shops

8 Wood waste is used for wood fires for heating

9 Organic waste is being composted

I think there must be more than this that we can do. The potential is there for us to recycle at least:

- Batteries
- Paint
- Cardboard

Cardboard is increasingly annoying. We have a huge collection of cardboard that I don't want to put out in the general trash that has now taken over the shed and the garage. We have been using some of it for the wood fires that we are using in order to reduce the oil consumption (we have free access to wood but unfortunately don't own an oilfield). I have tried to limit the cardboard from the shopping but it hasn't made that much of a difference. I can take it to the local recycling point, but that isn't an attractive option as the cardboard container there is always full, which isn't a big surprise because everyone else is getting just as much cardboard as I am, and they probably don't want it in their garage.

Some of the cardboard it seems can go in the compost as long as "it isn't too glossy" according to the literature. I'm not sure what would count as being too glossy so I am limiting it to brown cardboard at the moment. Of course, if I put all the cardboard in the compost bins I wouldn't have room for anything else, and it would undoubtedly disturb the delicate balance of greens and browns that I have been cultivating.

I can understand why the local authority doesn't want to collect it. It's cumbersome and doesn't weigh much, and when your waste targets are based on weight it makes far more sense to recycle glass and tin cans than it does cardboard. I am tempted to have a bonfire in the garden but that doesn't seem like the green option to me.

Also, like many people I have a huge and very rare collection of old paint tins in the garage, just in case I ever need to use them again. These are normally left there until they dry up completely at which point they find their way into the general rubbish. There is a recycling option with paint, which is to use the Community Repaint scheme, which aims to collect at least some of the estimated 80 million litres of unwanted paint that is sitting in garages over Britain, and give it free of charge to community groups and charities who have a need for it for painting community halls, youth clubs and the like. The Community Repaint website **www.communityrepaint.org.uk** has details of where local schemes are being operated.

Batteries are also a potentially significant recycling issue. Every year, 20,000 tonnes of batteries go to landfill sites in the UK. This equates to 300 million batteries every year[20] with the average household using 21 general purpose disposable batteries every year. Only 1,000 tonnes of batteries are currently recycled.[21]

There is a number of different types of household batteries, including:

- Wet-cell lead acid batteries used to power vehicles and by industry

- Dry-cell non-rechargeable: these are the most common types of household battery and include zinc carbon, zinc chloride and alkaline manganese

- There are also what they call primary button cells which can be mercury oxide (hearing aids, pacemakers), zinc air (hearing aids and radio pagers), silver oxide (watches and calculators) and lithium (watches and photographic equipment)

- Then there are all the dry-cell rechargeable batteries including nickel cadmium, nickel metal hydride and lithium-ion batteries used in power tools, cordless appliances, mobile phones, laptop computers and the like

Using rechargeable batteries reduces the number of batteries requiring disposal, but 80% of them contain nickel cadmium, a known human carcinogen, and therefore need to be disposed of safely[22]. It seems obvious that all of this going into landfill is not a great idea. Despite the fact that a lot of these batteries have a discreet label saying they should not be disposed of in the rubbish, this is where a lot of them end up.

The number of batteries in use is increasing all the time, with mobile phones, laptop computers, personal organisers and such being some of the most obvious users. But the primary button cells also seem to be finding their way into an ever increasing number of toys and books for children.

I have put an old ice cream container in the garage where all our batteries will now be stored until there is a sufficient number to be disposed of properly. After 10 days it has one AA battery in it, which doesn't seem to be much of a dent in 300 million going to landfill.

My enthusiasm is somewhat dampened by the information that it seems the only zinc processing plant in the UK closed down in 2003 and any batteries that need recycling have to go to France, Sweden or Switzerland to be recycled. I suppose that this isn't too surprising when based on the survey for this book 66% of people put their batteries in the general rubbish (although many of them made a note that they felt suitably guilty when they did so) and only 30% recycled them at local recycling centres. Most of the rest of us are apparently using an old ice cream container in the garage where, unsure of what to do with them, we are keeping our old batteries for obscure sentimental reasons.

In this second month I have also decided to try and address another green issue, and so I have started to think more carefully about the food miles involved in our weekly shopping exercise. Food miles are basically the number of miles that food has travelled before it reaches the dinner table. It seems that considering this to be six miles, which in our case is the distance between home and the supermarket, is not an accurate calculation.

As with many people our weekly shop is filled with products from far and distant lands that have travelled a significant number of miles, and in many cases look and taste as if they have as well. Of course it is impossible to really know how far any specific item has travelled in order to get to your local supermarket because it will have gone from processor to warehouse to retailer, which may well have necessitated several trips up and down the motorway, but at a basic level I think it's a pretty safe bet that anything that has travelled intercontinental has probably clocked up more food miles than something more locally produced. Most of the fruit and vegetables we buy have got gold cards and access to a complimentary lounge at the airport. I suspect that the majority of what we eat is still suffering from jet lag at the time when we're eating it. A quick analysis of this week's shop shows:

- Bananas – Ivory Coast
- Grapes – Spain
- Beans -- Kenya
- Cucumber – Spain
- Tomatoes – Spain
- Apples – New Zealand
- Sweet Potatoes – USA
- New Potatoes – Israel
- Dates – Israel
- Bacon – Denmark
- Mushrooms – Ireland
- Lettuce – Spain
- Onions – Spain
- Sweetcorn – Greece

- Carrots – UK
- Eggs – local farm

It's a veritable United Nations of fruit and vegetables. I am shocked by the fact that I seem to be eating sandwiches better travelled than I am, and that the only two UK products are carrots and eggs. I cannot imagine the kids eating a carrot omelette. To tell the truth I can't imagine eating a carrot omelette either.

The advice to eat locally grown produce is all very well as long as it's actually possible to buy it. My best chance of eating locally at the moment seems to be to move to Spain.

Although we are all very used to the range and selection of food from around the world, and the availability of whatever fresh fruit and vegetables we want regardless of the season, we have to acknowledge that environmentally this comes at a cost.

According to DEFRA food transportation has a social and environmental cost to the UK of £9 billion a year. It also accounts for 25% of all Heavy Goods Vehicle mileage in the UK. This was nearly nine billion vehicle kilometres in 2002[23], which explains why I seem to spend all my time on the road stuck behind a truck from one of the supermarkets. Food transport also emitted 10 million tonnes of carbon dioxide in the UK in 2002, which makes my 36 tonnes feel as if it is only a minor part of the problem.

Interestingly, if the UK average per household is about 10 tonnes per annum[24], and there are about 25 million households in the UK, this means that the total carbon dioxide emitted by households in the UK is about 250 million tonnes. Meanwhile, the transport of food around the UK is estimated to emit 10 million tonnes per annum. So the equivalent of 4% of all the carbon dioxide emitted by households in the UK is what we also produce by driving food around. Maybe eating locally produced food would help after all.

In order to make some immediate changes to the amount of food miles we generate, I decide to do the easy things first.

- Drink French wine instead of Australian

- Drink English bottled water instead of French

- Drink English beer (or beer brewed under licence in the UK) instead of French Lager

Is there no end to the sacrifices I am willing to make?

In an attempt to try and find more local food markets I have found an Internet directory of local food producers at **www.bigbarn.co.uk**. The website works brilliantly by allowing me to enter a postcode for which it will then produce me a map on which it shows the details of all the local food sources. Sadly, despite living in the middle of a farming area, there is little available. Within about 10 miles it shows:

- Two local 'farmer's markets' which (having already been to both of them) are notable only for the complete absence of any farmers (not that I'd want to buy one anyway)

- A local farm shop where it is possible to buy local meat and eggs (which I do anyway)

- A small flock of Alpacas producing very fine wool

- A supplier of wood chips

- A honey farm

Just for a moment I consider a diet of meat, eggs and honey, while dressing the kids in finest Alpaca.

Clearly more work is going to be required if I am going to be able to eat locally produced food.

As seems to be the case with most environmental decisions it is most likely that there is insufficient information available ever to be completely sure of any decision I make. If sufficient information is available it will almost certainly contain diametrically opposed conclusions. For example, it is possible that food miles may be the lesser of two evils. It is possible that the environmental impact of local farming methods is more damaging than the impact of the miles travelled in order for food produced using sustainable environmentally friendly farming methods to reach me. Or it may be that by consuming these imported goods I may be helping to sustain poor peasant farmers who would otherwise have no market for what they produce. Or then again, perhaps buying these goods is forcing these farmers to produce a cash crop for export while the local population doesn't have enough to eat. I don't know, and the chances are that nobody else really knows either, but on the basis that the miles travelled is something I can comprehend, it is probably the better environmental basis on which to try and buy my food.

Then again, buying food from local farmers, allegedly rich beyond the dreams of avarice from European Union subsidy doesn't seem right, when I could be buying it from a peasant farmer somewhere in the third world, who depends on his exports of mange tout to earn a meagre living and feed his family. I am in a quandary and all because I bought green beans from Kenya.

This is getting much too hard for me.

Just when all hope seems to be lost; it seems there is a local company called The Ethical Food Company, which will deliver local, organic, and ethical foodstuffs to the doorstep. Unfortunately there are two major problems with this. Firstly, it falls foul of my 5% rule, in that the prices are significantly higher than those available from the supermarket. Secondly the contents are likely to be a problem. The typical contents list includes pointed cabbage, broad beans, beetroot, baby spinach, chard, cauliflower, calabrese and asparagus. Of these, only cauliflower is something the kids will eat, and even then only under protest. Also, as a rule, I only tend to eat something if I know what it is. Calabrese and chard would both fail that test as well. This is a shame, and perhaps our eating habits are one of the things that will have to change if there is to be any greener lifestyle.

Unfortunately, there seem to be several areas where my eating habits may need to change, depending on who I listen to.

1 We should eat locally produced food to reduce the carbon emissions associated with the transport of food

2 We should eat food when it is in season. In some ways this is a natural corollary of eating locally produced food, but it would also seem to exclude locally produced food that uses production techniques designed to extend the growing season

3 We should become vegetarians because it uses less of the Earth's resources to produce vegetables than it does to produce the food for animals to eat in order for us to then eat the meat

4 We should eat the food that produces the most nutritional value for the least amount of resources required for its production. This, by the way, means no more lettuce

5 We should eat organic food in order to reduce the pesticides and chemicals that are pumped into the food chain

6 We should eat fair trade food because it helps farmers in the developing world

Unfortunately some of these seem to be mutually exclusive. Food in the supermarket may be organic, but it almost certainly isn't local. Organic food is not necessarily green food if it has travelled thousands of miles to get to me. Local food may not be organic, but at least it hasn't circumnavigated the world. Fair trade food has almost certainly travelled at least intercontinentally, but it may be a valid ethical decision regardless.

Sadly, this seems to be another green issue where the problem is bigger than the solutions that are available. As a society we are used to the availability of cheap and varied food through the convenience of the supermarket shelves and a trolley with its own bizarre sense of direction. As a result of this and the food sourcing practices that enable the supermarkets to achieve it, the opportunity to eat locally produced food is limited to those who have the ability to find local suppliers and are willing to give up the convenience of one large supermarket shop every week.

In the survey for this book only 8% always bought local food, although another 84% sometimes bought local produce. The reasons for not buying local food produce more often were:

- 40% said they shopped in a supermarket for convenience

- 35% said the food they wanted to buy wasn't available as local produce

- 16% said the price of local produce was the limiting factor for them

These reasons for not buying local produce were very different from the reasons given for not buying organic produce. These were:

- 62% said the price of organic food stopped them buying more of it. A number of people also expressed a lot of suspicion that the price of organic food is being artificially inflated by the suppliers

- 31% said that the food they wanted to buy was not available as organic produce

- 8% said that they were suspicious of organic claims, particularly when it is imported organic food

- 4% said the quality of organic food was not good enough

- 15% said they would buy non-organic local food rather than organic

(I know this adds up to more than 100%, this is because a lot of respondents gave multiple reasons for not buying organic food.)

All this despite the fact that being organic is one of the most promoted ways of being greener and reducing your intake of pesticide residue and encouraging organic farming methods that, at some point, will hopefully reduce the number of chemicals pumped into the countryside in an attempt to achieve the greatest level of subsidy.

So, with a brisk step and an optimistic outlook I went to the supermarket to check out the organic fare that is on offer. Bearing in mind the fact that I am only prepared to pay a 5% premium to be greener, this was a waste of the six miles worth of carbon dioxide that the journey pumped into the atmosphere. I was shocked and awed. Some simple price comparisons left me shocked that people actually buy this stuff, and awed that someone was smart enough to realise they could sell it at that price.

The table below shows the price differential for a range of products. The comparison ignores any special price reductions or buy one get one free offers (of which there were distressingly few) and did not include the 'value' option for any of the non-organic products. The products were selected pretty much at random and with no omissions just to allow me to prove a point (I promise).

Product	Organic Price Differential
Carrots	+ 47%
Potatoes	+93%
New Potatoes	+68%
Apples	+71%
Tomatoes	+96%
Sweet Pointed Peppers	+72%
Bell Peppers	+82%
Celery	+43%
Little Gem Lettuce	+71%
Romaine Lettuce	+11%
Bananas	+32%
Mushrooms	+10%
Sweetheart Cabbage	+87%
Cauliflower	+87%
Orange Juice	+109%
Flour	+68%
Coffee	+56%
Tea Bags	+28%
Milk	+25%

I suspect I may be in the wrong business. I just don't know whether I should be a supermarket or an organic farmer, but one thing's for sure, with price differentials like this, somebody's having a laugh at the expense of everyone who thinks they're making a sensible choice by eating organic food. (With the honourable exception of anyone who's growing their own organic produce in the garden.)

Also noticeable were all the strange packaging coincidences that could catch out the unwary shopper with a tinge of green as they wander round the supermarket. For example:

- A good number of organic goods are packaged in a different measure from non-organic. For example, organic was a bag of six apples, while non-organic was a bag of seven apples. Bell peppers were packaged as two for organic and three for non-organic

- There were instances where the price of the organic package was almost identical to the non-organic package, but the measures were different

Now, if I was cynical about this, I would suspect that some of this was a deliberate ploy. But of course I have no doubt whatsoever that it couldn't possibly be anything other than an unfortunate coincidence. I have checked the thesaurus and it has no reference to organic as a synonym for profiteering. However, from now on I will not have any difficulty in feeling fully justified as I bypass anything labelled organic.

As an organic aside, there is also the issue of organic clothes to consider. 85% of the people surveyed for this book had never bought organic clothes. I have to confess that I was more surprised to find that there were 15% who claimed to buy organic clothes, including the 1.6% who claimed always to buy organic clothes. The reasons given for not buying organic clothes were given as:

- 40% of the people surveyed had no idea there was such a thing as organic clothes

- 35% said the range and availability put them off buying them

- 6% said the price put them off

Having had an (admittedly very cursory) look at whether we should think about buying organic clothes for the children I think a lot more people would find the price a reason for not buying them once they had heard of them and knew where to buy them. Just as with organic food, for me, the price to the consumer has got to be at least comparable before I am going to be wearing anything hemp based.

Things aren't going so well with the electricity. Even after my initial attempts to reduce the amount of electricity we use overnight, I am still concerned by the number of things that are switched on overnight and using power. After our initial cull of these appliances we still have.

1 1 television signal booster installed in the loft
2 1 Digibox on standby
3 1 Freeview box on standby
4 1 television on standby
5 4 hands-free telephones on chargers

6 1 fax machine

7 1 telephone answering machine

8 1 septic tank pump

9 1 60W outside light on a timer until 11pm

10 3 night lights for the kids

11 1 microwave

12 2 CD players on stand by

13 1 radio alarm

14 2 Freezers

15 2 Fridges

16 1 dustbuster on charge

17 1 DVD player on standby

18 1 VCR on standby

19 1 baby monitor

20 2 mains wired smoke alarms (as mandated by building regulations)

21 1 alarm system

Despite being aware of the problem it seems that I haven't done that much about it. So to try and reduce the overnight electricity usage I have now:

• Reorganised the fridges so that one is no longer required

• Turned the dustbuster off permanent charge

• Cut down the amount of time the outside light is on with the timer

• Changed round the plugs so that the television, DVD, VCR and the Digibox can be switched off easily

- Changed the nightly routine so that I switch off the kid's CD players when I go to bed

The majority of the other items I can do nothing about. They need to be on overnight.

Some more analysis of the problem seems to suggest that even when some items are switched off they seem to be draining power somehow.

Part of the problem is still in the way in which we have got all these electrical items plugged into the wall. We have a number of strip plugs that have multiple devices attached to them, some of which I want to have switched on all the time and others which I want to be able to switch off when they are not being used. As they are all plugged into the same strip plug, nothing gets switched off at all.

I have now reconfigured everything that can be switched off at the wall in such a way that they are separate from the electronics I still want to be left on overnight (telephones for example). By doing this I can quickly switch everything off at the plug every evening. In the one area of the house where this isn't possible, I have swapped the strip plug for one where there are individual switches for each socket.

The effects of these actions are almost instantaneous. Our overnight power consumption has gone down from 11 kilowatt hours to just eight. I have saved the best part of 30 pence a day, which in real money is £110 a year, just by switching things off at the wall.

Despite this minor success, I have to admit I am becoming

increasingly confused and frustrated by the sheer number of things that I apparently ought to be doing in order to be considered green. I am even more confused and frustrated by the number of things that I should not be doing in order to be considered to be living a greener lifestyle. Rather than just proclaim this to be too hard for me and give up, I have been thinking of a way in which I can manage this.

I have decided to categorise all green activities into primary and secondary green issues.

Primary green issues are those where it is my direct action that impacts the environment. Secondary issues are those where my choices effect someone else's environmental impact. So, for example, recycling my wine bottles would be a primary green activity, while buying food that has been grown locally would be a secondary green activity on the basis that the environmental cost of the transport of the food I buy has been created by somebody else. So there are areas of my life where I can change my own impact on the environment, and then there are choices I can make in order to try and influence the environmental impact of others.

This may only be an exercise in self-delusion, but if it stops me having a complete nervous breakdown over my impact on the environment, I for one believe it has some significant value. So, primary activities include:

- Reducing overall consumption

- Reducing electricity consumption

- Reducing number of miles driven in the car

- Recycling whatever can be recycled (glass, paper, plastics, clothes, shoes etc)

- Reducing the amount of waste produced

- Using environmentally friendly products such as washing up liquid, washing powder etc

- Reducing water usage

- Buying green gifts

Secondary activities would include:

- Buying locally produced food in order to reduce the environmental impact of food transport

- Investing any savings in green investments in order to encourage green business activities. (Fortunately this isn't a big issue for me as I haven't got any money, but I can dream)

- Switching to a green energy supplier in order to encourage the use of renewables for energy production

The primary activities have a much more immediate level of satisfaction associated with them as it is possible to see the difference, even if nobody else does anything. The secondary activities which require my actions to have an influence on the actions of huge multi-billion pound corporations are somewhat more difficult to get excited about. However, as some of them may have a major impact on how my life is perceived by carbon footprint calculators I may well consider them anyway. However, it is difficult enough to worry about what I am doing environmentally without worrying about everyone else as well.

This, in a nutshell, seems to be the fundamental problem with trying to go green; any real change depends upon everybody (or at least a majority) of people doing it. This applies to both the primary and secondary activities, but as an individual I am resigned to the fact that recycling my newspapers isn't going to stop somebody cutting down vast swathes of rain forest, and buying local produce isn't going to stop supermarket trucks racing up and down the motorway. In terms of saving the planet my own actions are pretty futile which, I suspect, is almost certainly why a lot of people don't bother.

If, however, we all did it, it really would make a difference at least to the government's ability to claim they are meeting their commitments on carbon emissions, if not to anything else.

CHAPTER 3

Month three

"I don't want to look sad."

One reason given for not buying organic clothes.

It will soon be Christmas, which in our house, as in many others is a time of over indulgence, excessive consumption, and general wastefulness. My suggestion that we do without lights on the Christmas tree is greeted with howls of derision from my wife, and screams of despair from two small children who are concerned as to exactly how Santa is going to identify where they live. A green Christmas is going to be more difficult than I thought it would be and as Christmas approaches it seems that this is not a time of good will as far as the environment is concerned.

The joy of sending 1.7 billion Christmas Cards is at the expense of chopping down 200,000 trees, and then another 40,000 to make the wrapping paper for the gifts. I have thought about sending an e-card as an environmentally friendly option that uses nothing more than a bit of spare computing power somewhere. There are only three problems with this plan.

- Firstly, 95% of the people I send a card to wouldn't know what to do with an e-card unless I printed it out and put it in the post to them

- Secondly, the only times I have received e-cards my first thought has not been to congratulate the sender on their environmental friendliness but to berate them for having forgotten my birthday and being too cheap to buy a proper card

- Thirdly, every time I have received an e-card this has been the precursor to a several thousand percent increase in the volume of spam received. Personally I take offense at the implication that it is too small or that I should be taking little blue pills on a regular basis

We throw out an additional three million tons of waste, and send six million Christmas trees to landfill sites. This sounds like a much nicer gesture than it really is. Our house has a plastic Christmas tree, which I suspect isn't a good thing, but we have had it for 15 years so it can't be that bad – most of the decorations are 15 years old as well.

I contemplate buying everyone an ethical Christmas present. I could plant a tree, buy a goat for a family in the developing world, or then again I could choose not to have two screaming children on Christmas morning asking me why Santa brought them a farm animal when what they really wanted was something made of plastic with batteries in it.

Personally I am tempted to adopt a turtle through the Marine Conservation Society[25]. I threaten the kids that I will register them with the alternative Christmas gift website for any gifts from relatives, rather than taking the time to explain the specifics of the awful computer game they want to their grand-parents[26].

I have however cancelled all plans for a large flashing Santa on the roof. I wasn't going to have one anyway, but it makes me feel better if I think I'm denying myself something I really wanted.

Then, of course, there is Christmas dinner. The ingredients for a typical Christmas dinner may have travelled as many as 30,000 miles from producers and growers to the UK dinner table and a combination of European turkeys, African vegetables, Australian wine and American cranberry sauce will have notched up enough food miles between them to have earned hot and cold running stewardesses and a free ticket for their spouse the next time they fly anywhere.

The biggest problem with Christmas is that this seems to be the time when the most green preaching is undertaken, thus leading to the popular conception that in order to be green you have to be as miserable as sin, an utter and complete kill joy, and quite possibly deficient in key areas of brain function. Christmas is when some of the green organisations feel com-pelled to impart their most annoying advice. For example:

1 For Christmas decorations: "Collect up empty packages, scraps of fabric, wool, old cards, paints, scissors and glue – get friends or family round the table and let your creativity flow."[27] In our house this stuff is what is known as 'rubbish',

and putting our family around the table with scissors and glue is only going to lead to an unnecessary trip to the emergency department

2 As a hangover cure: "...the best veggie hangover cure is a banana milkshake, made from soya milk, honey and ground almonds and of course bananas." I may never drink again

On Christmas day I make a vague attempt to try and ensure we will be able to reuse the wrapping paper. Unfortunately a five year old and a two year old interpret 'don't rip the paper' as 'please tear it to shreds in your excitement so that it can never be used again'.

However, we have done a few things that cost nothing (in the grand scheme of things) and help to make Christmas slightly less environmentally damaging than it could have been otherwise.

- We have minimised the number of toys that need to have batteries. And where batteries are required we have ensured we have rechargeable ones available

- Christmas dinner is based mainly on seasonal produce from the UK. It is a good thing we all like parsnips. The turkey was local as well. It's probably one of the only environmentally good things that Christmas has got going for it that the traditional Christmas dinner is based mainly on seasonally available produce (as long as we ignore the imported desire for cranberry sauce)

- We have not gone on a cheap flight to somewhere warm for

the Christmas break. I quite like this, because it is now possible to feel good about not doing something I wasn't going to do anyway. The point is that I could have gone on a cheap flight and I didn't, and that's got to be good for the environment

- We eat leftovers for three days after Christmas

Even trying our best, however, the wheelie bin is still bursting at the seams by the time Christmas is over. I comfort myself that, bad as it is, this is still a lot better than it usually is at this time of year, and fall asleep in front of the television watching 'The Great Escape'.

CHAPTER 4

Month four

It feels as if we've reached something of a plateau already in the attempt to be greener. I have trouble believing that it can be as simple as it seems to be. It is almost as if there is only a base level of advice consisting of turning the thermostat down, buying some low wattage light bulbs, and recycling the basics, and once you've done all that then there isn't much left for an individual to do, unless you want to get into the area of alternative lifestyles.

It may be the case that those giving the advice don't think that the rest of us are capable of much more than the basics, so why confuse us with anything more complicated? Or it might be that if they could get us all to do just the basics it would be more than they ever expected.

From the survey it seems that the areas where there has been a significant amount of promotion and publicity are now relatively well accepted. Recycling for example showed that:

- 98% of people claimed they recycled their newspapers. The remaining 2% were using it for pet bedding (not a result I expected), which is reuse rather than recycling but just as good

- 99% claimed they recycled glass bottles

- 85% recycled cardboard

- 77% recycled plastics

- 77% recycled tin cans

These are the main items that we generally think about for recycling as they seem to be the most common items collected by local authorities, and the materials that have received the most recycling promotion.

When we move onto the items that receive less attention from a recycling standpoint, the numbers change quite dramatically.

- Only 16% recycled paint
- Only 30% recycled batteries

The fact that they are lower use items and don't have any doorstep collection makes it less convenient to recycle them and the majority of these items end up in the general rubbish. It seems that the key to being green is to make it easy and to make it into a habit where the more environmentally friendly action becomes the default, rather than the exception.

It is this that makes me think that the reason why people aren't greener than they could be is not down to a lack of desire to be green, but it is the fact that the desire to be green doesn't outweigh the desire for convenience.

If we take green electricity for example (buying electricity that has been produced from a renewable source such as wind, wave, solar, or hydroelectric) only 30% had a considered reason why they had not switched, these being mainly cost and a scepticism about how environmentally friendly green electricity really was. The majority of responses were to do with lack of knowledge or lack of time to consider it.

- 24% didn't know there was such a thing as green electricity

- 16% just "hadn't thought about it"
- 9% were too lazy to switch

So the main reasons why people said they weren't using green electricity were due to lack of knowledge and the time to consider it and make the switch.

Perhaps the reason why I feel as if we have reached a plateau is because many of the things I thought would be difficult to do are starting to become a habit rather than an effort.

However, despite this, we are still using more electricity than I think we should be, which I still need to get to the bottom of. As I continually try to work out why our electricity consumption is still well above the national average it has become clear that, as with many aspects of life, the fact that my wife and I both work from home a lot is an environmentally mixed blessing. On the positive side there is that:

- Neither of us incurs any environmental cost from commuting

- We don't consume electricity at the office or any office space

On the negative side

- We consume a significant amount of electricity at home through the computers, printers, lights, and regular caffeine intake

- We produce more waste at home, particularly as printed paper

My estimate is that the home working aspect of our lives accounts for about four kilowatt hours of electricity per day, which I estimate as mainly being two computers and the kettle. Overall it is believed that working from home is much more environmentally friendly as:

- It cuts out the transport costs

- The energy efficiency of homes is normally rather better than the energy efficiency of office buildings, particularly in terms of heating large office spaces. People working in an office consume more energy per person than someone working from home

However, although it is the best choice from an environmental perspective, it does also have the effect of distorting our electricity consumption to make it look as if we are worse than we really are. That's my story and I'm sticking to it.

The issue of more waste is more difficult to deal with. There is all the additional waste from eating lunch at home rather than in the office and the significant amount of paper that still seems to be produced, despite the promise of a paperless office. In order to try and reduce the amount of paper waste we produce we are doing simple things like reusing paper that has only been printed on one side and I have also set up a recycling box in the corner (just like in the office) for paper that has been completely used. Sadly, this box doesn't come with contract cleaning staff to empty it in the evening. Our total office waste is about half a bin bag a week, which is now about 30% of our total waste produced. Interestingly we both find ourselves less likely to consume resources at home, in particular printing things rather than reading them on the screen. I think that this is purely psychological in that it feels as if we are using our own resources at home, so we are naturally somewhat more careful with them.

Of course working at home has some other environmental effects.

1 The ironing is significantly reduced from the time when it was a shirt and tie every day

2 Expenditure on clothes and shoes for work has reduced to zero

3 The garden is better looked after, with more home produce as a result

Overall while I believe the net effect of working at home on a day to day basis is beneficial to the environment, it does serve to make the house seem less environmentally friendly than would be the case if it was empty all day. Of course, as seems to be the case with all things environmental there are alternative views about whether working from home generally is an environmentally good thing as:

- It may encourage people to move into larger homes and so encourage urban sprawl and greater costs per person in heating and lighting due to the increased size of the home

- It may encourage expenditure on office related products (desk lamps, filing cabinets, executive leather chairs, and so on)

- It may encourage people to live further away from a workplace they do have to visit at some point in the week, and so add to transport costs

Once again, nobody really seems to know whether it's a good thing or a bad thing. In my particular case, it may overall have been a bad thing for the environment as we had to extend the house in order to cater for home working.

CHAPTER 5

Month five

"My husband's too lazy to switch"

One reason for not switching to a green electricity provider.

Well, we have blown any green credentials at all by going on holiday to America. In order to make up for the greenhouse gases emitted by a 777 it seems I will need to drink two and a half billion bottles of wine and recycle all the glass. I intend to try.

However, it seems that my belief that aviation is the curse of the climate may be mistaken, and it is possible I have been the victim of misinformation. According to British Airways (**www.britishairways.com**) aviation is responsible for only 2% of the man-made carbon dioxide emissions and 5% of the UK's carbon dioxide emissions. Aviation may not be the big bad wolf of climate change after all, and although it may be the fastest growing source of emissions, this is probably a statistical fact only because it is growing from a very small base. There are other considerations, in that carbon dioxide emissions aren't aviation's only possible contribution to global warming, but it seems that the science is unclear as to the impact of aviation on the formation of ozone in the troposphere. However, when considering flights as a contributor to the total emissions of the UK there doesn't seem to be as much need to suffer holiday guilt as some would have us believe. This is something of a relief to me, but bad news for the French wine industry.

It is also possible to pay to offset the effects of the flight via the British Airways website, which for four of us would have been £59 to cover the 7.06 tonnes of carbon dioxide we apparently emitted as a result of the journey. I have to admit I passed on this opportunity, but resolved to plant two apple trees in the garden to make up for it.

Once again, this seems to show the lack of reliable and in some cases even honest information that is available to make personal decisions on actions that may impact the climate.

One of the actions I have been meaning to take for some time is to switch our electricity to a green electricity plan. Fortunately this doesn't involve running pylons from the nearest wind farm to my back door. In fact, even if I switch to a green provider, there would be no change to the way in which electricity is fed into the house. I would just get a bill from a different company.

Although it is the same electricity I would be using as I am using today, for every unit I use, the electricity provider will ensure that they source the same amount from a green electricity source. The website **www.uswitch.com** provides an online automated mechanism for switching providers, and also comparing prices. This is something of a shock. The most obvious green plan on there is 12% more expensive for secondary units used and more than 50% more expensive for primary units used. If this is their idea of a joke it's not a funny one. This would cost me the best part of another £150 a year, and I apologise profusely, but that's just not going to happen. Ironically, however, if I switched to a green electricity plan, this does make the domestic wind turbine option more financially viable, although I'm pretty sure that wasn't their intention.

Telephoning my existing electricity provider is no more satisfying. I am told that their green electricity product is currently under review and unavailable to new customers until their replacement product is launched. Somewhere there is probably a product manager wondering why his green product isn't doing very well.

More by chance than anything I have discovered a company called ecotricity (**www.ecotricity.com**) who promise to match the rate of your existing electricity provider. It was remarkably easy to switch suppliers using the Internet, and I also spoke to their customer services on the telephone who were very helpful. What's more, everything still seems to be working and we haven't had a power cut yet. It is a nice feeling to know that the carbon emissions from the electricity usage in the house are now zero. I have filled the kettle to celebrate. I am choosing to block out the thought that I am now partly responsible for huge wind turbines sprouting up across areas of previously unspoilt countryside.

To be honest, I'm not sure why I prevaricated about doing this for so long. It is an easy thing to do and theoretically makes an immediate impact. It will also significantly change the way in which the carbon footprint calculators view my impact on the planet, and (again theoretically) makes it unnecessary for me to install a wind turbine on top of the house.

Three days later however I have still not received the promised confirmation email that shows the switch has taken place. It seems that the ecotricity website wasn't working properly when I decided to switch.

In the UK, electricity is generated from a variety of sources. Gas accounts for 39%, Coal 35%, Nuclear 20% and Renewables 4%. There is a target for 20% to be from renewables by 2016. The sources of renewable energy are also many and varied, and include:

- Onshore wind turbines
- Offshore wind turbines
- Energy crops (biomass)
- Solar power
- Hydroelectricity
- Geothermal power
- Wave power
- Tidal Power
- Landfill gas
- Sewage gas
- Waste incineration

Of course, as always seems to be the case when trying to make a green choice, the decision to use a renewable energy source isn't without its problems. Unfortunately, just as moving to Spain seems to be the only way to reduce food miles, moving to Iceland seems to be the only way to acquire renewable energy, due to the availability of geothermal power.

All forms of renewable energy production seem to have some impact on the environment[28]. For example,

- Onshore wind has the visual impact of turbine, the impact of building concrete footings for turbines, the impact of pylons to distribute electricity, noise pollution from the turbines and additional access roads required to the turbines

- Offshore wind has the visual impact of turbines, the damage to sea bed and marine life, and the onshore cables and equipment required to link to the National Grid

- Wind power can have a significant impact on wildlife, especially birds and bats that have a tendency to be surprised by the presence of huge rotating blades in the middle of the countryside. One of the clearest examples of this has been the impact of a Norwegian wind farm on the local population of White Tailed Eagles, where nine eagles were killed in 10 months including almost all of the chicks born in that year[29]

- Biomass has the impact on biodiversity of mass planting of a single crop, the impact on fields and hedgerows, the impact on wildlife, the carbon emissions from burning biomass fuels and the impact of transporting energy crops and additional fuel

- Solar power has the visual impact of solar panels

- Hydroelectric power has the impact on the ecology of the water environment, river flow and the like, and the impact of access roads to the turbines

- Wave Power has the impact of access roads to onshore equipment, the impact to the sea bed and marine environment, and the impact of onshore cables and equipment linking it to the National grid

Basically, any way you look at it, it might be renewable, but to imagine it has no environmental impact is a bit like me imagining I am particularly witty after two bottles of wine (i.e. wishful thinking).

However, regardless of the arguments of the possible environmental impacts of green power generation, the survey conducted for this book showed that:

- 9% of those surveyed claimed to be receiving their electricity from a green electricity provider

- 5% were considering switching to a green electricity provider

Of those who were not getting their electricity delivered from a green provider, the reasons they gave for not doing so were:

- 24% said that they either didn't know such an option existed, or they didn't know who the providers were

- 16% said they had just not thought about it

- 14% said that it was too expensive

- 10% were sceptical about the benefits of switching to a green provider

- 9% admitted to being too lazy to switch

- 4% said they could not switch for some reason, for example they were living in rented shared accommodation

- 9% gave no reason for not using a green provider

So there would seem to be a huge opportunity for more people to switch to renewable electricity providers and so boost the emphasis on renewables as opposed to nuclear power generation. It does, by the way, feel like a very strange world when nuclear power can be presented as the most environmentally friendly option available to us. Perhaps I'm just old fashioned and don't want my children to glow in the dark.

CHAPTER 6

Month six

"Overpriced, overhyped nonsense, delivering marginal benefit"

"A well off middle class fad."

Comments on organic food from survey research.

I think I am starting to suffer from what I can only describe as 'green fatigue'. I don't seem to be able to turn on the television or open a newspaper without seeing alarmist rants on the state of the planet. For some reason I get the impression it's my fault. The more green I try to be, the higher my eco-guilt levels seem to go. I am also getting tired of switching lights off behind the rest of the family, avoiding the more tempting and highly packaged items on display in the supermarket, living in a house full of drying clothes and, most of all, I am sick of washing up tin cans. Generally, (and I freely admit that this may be a case of some self-justification here) I am also becoming increasingly suspicious of green claims. This seems to be confirmed by some of the responses to the survey. Many people were concerned about the effectiveness of fair trade, especially with countries where child labour may be involved anyway, the food miles involved in ensuring the availability of organic products, and a strong perception that both organic and fair trade product prices reflect price gouging by suppliers. Wind farms and green energy were also the subject of particularly negative comments.

I also suspect that most of what I am doing is, at best, a futile gesture. At worst, it doesn't even rate being considered a futile gesture. The more I look into what can be achieved by an individual householder, the less it seems worth doing it. As an example, the one area that I have been most pleased with is our ability to reduce the amount of wheelie bin space we consume on a weekly basis. Unfortunately, I then made the mistake of looking at the statistics for waste available from DEFRA, and the sources of waste in the UK are as follows:

- Construction and demolition: 32%
- Mining and quarrying: 29%
- Industrial: 14%
- Commercial: 11%
- Household: 9%
- Dredged materials: 5%
- Agricultural: < 1%
- Sewage Sludge: < 1%

So, if all the households in the UK cut their waste production by 50% this would reduce the overall UK waste production by 4.5%. If the construction and demolition industry cut their waste production by just 14% this would have the same effect on overall waste[30]. It is not surprising that as an individual householder it hardly seems worth bothering.

Given that there are about to be fines imposed on local authorities for excess waste sent to land fill, it would seem that something sensible has to be done about waste in the very near future.

In a fit of enthusiasm for the waste issue I looked at the waste strategy for our local authority to see what they were going to do to avoid the landfill fines. There is no doubt from the document that waste is likely to be an even bigger problem in the future unless something is done. The local authorities' specific plans include:

1 Refurbishment of existing recycling centres

2 Introduction of new recycling centres

3 Trial of an organic collection service for green waste and cardboard

4 Development of new composting centres

5 Further campaigns to encourage recycling

This is based on an analysis of the waste that is produced (after recycling and composting) which shows it to be 70% biodegradable. This is a major problem with landfill in that it is estimated that the methane produced by landfill sites accounts for about 2% of the UK's methane emissions. (Methane of course being a gas that is particularly bad for global warming.)

Unfortunately, even with these actions in place, there seems to be little doubt that what the local authority somewhat coyly refers to as "an alternative to landfill" will be required. This is described as "Advanced Thermal Treatment", or "pyrolysis" and "gasification". They can call it what they like, it basically means they're going to burn it. So, The European Union Landfill directive, designed (presumably) to try and protect the environment and make a positive contribution to reducing greenhouse gas emissions by reducing the methane emitted from landfill sites, is going to result in household waste being burned across the country.

There is a huge additional irony here in that once the investment is made in incineration facilities (sorry, Advanced Thermal Treatment) it is then necessary to ensure there is enough waste produced to keep the facility viable. It is quite possible that these facilities actually encourage waste.

It's no wonder that I'm suffering from green fatigue. It's like squeezing a balloon. Wherever you try and do something to improve the environment or be greener, somewhere else it seems to cause a negative impact. So in the same way as fining local authorities for landfill will make them burn more waste, if you buy organic food it turns out it travelled 20,000 miles in order to get to you. If you buy green electricity it turns out that you're personally responsible for a thousand huge wind turbines spread across an area of outstanding natural beauty. If you put in double glazing it turns out that the process of making that double glazing created enough emissions to heat the house without double glazing for the next thousand years.

Increasingly it seems to me that, in exactly the same way that by the time I was sitting in the kitchen wondering what to do with all the food packaging, thinking about waste once it has been produced is too late in the process. Somehow, waste has got to be managed out of the system at source. We have to try and get to the point at which we can achieve zero waste.

Again, there is a huge irony here in that the relative success of recycling may actually serve to make us complacent about reducing consumption in the first place. Everything seems to be alright as long as it is recycled. None of this takes into account the cost of production or the cost of recycling and yet it sends a general message that encourages consumption and recycling that applies to all goods, despite the fact there is so much for which recycling capabilities don't exist.

The idea of achieving zero waste is one that for some reason I have started to find intrinsically appealing. There is (inevitably) a pressure group designed to promote this, and according to the Zero Waste Alliance, the concept of zero waste entails redesigning products and changing the way waste is handled, so products last longer, materials are recycled, or, in the case of organics, composted. Waste is effectively designed out of the process. Their 10 point plan for achieving this in the UK is:

- Set a target of Zero Waste for all municipal waste in Britain by 2020 (50% by 2010 and 75% by 2015)

- Extend the doorstep collection of dry recyclables to every home in Britain without delay

- Provide doorstep collection of organic waste, and establish a network of local closed vessel compost plants

- Convert civic amenity sites into reuse and recycling centres

- Ban from 2006 the landfilling of biological waste, which has not been treated and neutralised

- Ban any new thermal treatment of mixed waste and limit disposal contracts to a maximum of 10 years

- Extend the Landfill Tax into a disposal tax. Increase its level, and use it to fund the Zero Waste programmes

- Extend Producer Responsibility legislation to all products/materials that are hazardous or difficult to recycle

- Open up waste planning to greater public participation and end the commercial confidentiality of waste contracts

- Establish a Zero Waste Agency to promote resource efficiency and act as a guardian of public health[31]

This would all seem eminently sensible to me.

The ability of the homeowner to have a significant impact on electricity usage is also limited. Domestic users represent only about a third of all electricity consumed in the UK. The majority of the rest is consumed by business of some sort[32]. Forty four percent of the UK's carbon emissions are from industrial and commercial sources[33]. Again, it doesn't look as if the average householder is where all the blame should lie.

On the positive side, I am also fairly pleased with the results of putting some thought into when I use the car and using one journey to accomplish two or three things rather than three journeys to accomplish not much. My monthly mileage seems to have stabilised at about 370 miles per month, which would give an annual mileage of 4,450 miles. This is down from my usual annual mileage of about 8,500 miles; a reduction of nearly 48% or 4,050 miles. My estimate of the car's fuel consumption is that it currently costs me about 14 pence per mile just in petrol. In six months I have saved somewhere around £283 in petrol costs alone. Despite the fact that this does not seem to be reflected in an ever improving bank balance, this is still good news. Unfortunately my car is only one of 27 million registered cars in the UK, so it is unlikely that I am making a significant difference on my own. Increasingly it seems to me that the best motivation for adopting a greener lifestyle is one of enlightened self-interest, rather than any desire to save the planet or change the course of climate change.

For some time now I have let the electricity usage continue at its new level of somewhere between 28 and 30 kilowatt hours per day. This is something like a 35% reduction from our pre-green days, but I am painfully aware that it is still not very good. The base level of electricity usage in the house still seems to be high. When we went on vacation the house somehow managed to continue to use 12 kilowatt hours per day without anybody actually living here. This feels like a lot of electricity to be used by an empty house.

A little bit of research however has shown that there is (what their marketing suggests) an amazing little device that can be connected to the outside wire from the meter to give a very precise reading of the amount of electricity being used.

My attempts to order this are frustrated by the fact that on the first telephone call I get an answering machine message telling me that they are all on holiday, on the second attempt I get an answering machine message telling me that they are away from their desk, and on the third attempt it seems that they are unable to receive incoming telephone calls. This is not filling me with confidence. However, given the level of underlying electricity consumption in the house, I am not giving up and so I have ordered online at **www.electrisave.com**. This proves to be a lot easier than trying to call them.

To my relief the device turns up the next day, so like a kid with a new toy, I have already connected it to the electricity supply (it just slips around the wire rather than being connected into it, which means I didn't need to call out an electrician to do this). The whole process of setting it up took less than five minutes, and I am now sitting staring at the screen which shows me how much money I am spending on electricity. This is more annoying than I could possibly imagine, so I have been walking round the house switching things off and seeing what they are costing me. At a rate per kilowatt hour of 14.4 pence the following shocking discoveries are made.

1 The house is operating at a cost of 14.9 pence per hour, despite the fact I'm not doing anything other than using the computer

2 Leaving the TV on standby upstairs is costing me 0.7 pence per hour

3 The fact that the kids didn't turn off the light in the bathroom is costing me 3 pence per hour

4 The fridge costs 3.8 pence an hour to run

5 Opening the fridge door costs an additional 0.3 pence per hour

6 Boiling the kettle with three cups of water in it costs 39.4 pence per hour

7 The freezer costs 4.1 pence per hour

(I admit I'm in danger of becoming a bit of an anorak about this.)

There were some things that I was sure would make a difference but didn't:

1 Turning off a computer monitor that was on standby

2 Switching the cooker off at the wall switch

The main problem is that most of our appliances are 10 years old (or more) and were bought at a time when an energy rating better than 'C' meant another £100 added to the purchase price. As a result, we don't have many 'A' rated appliances. For future purchases though, the Energy Saving Trust (**www.est.org.uk**) has a database of electrical appliances that are the best for saving energy.

Having discovered just how much power the kettle actually uses, and with my new electrisave device now turning me into a home appliance trainspotter, I have been able to answer a question that has been bothering me for some time. Which is better – coffee machine or kettle?

Our coffee machine provides about six mugs of coffee. If I drink a mug every half an hour while I am working, this means that the coffee machine would be on for three hours or I would be boiling the kettle six times.

The coffee machine goes through an initial burst as it is heating the water when it uses 0.77 kilowatts per hour for about eight minutes. After that it uses approximately 0.24 kilowatts to keep the coffee warm. So three hours' worth of coffee machine would use eight minutes at 0.103 kilowatts plus 0.24 x 3 (0.72 kilowatt hours) giving a total of 0.823 kilowatt hours for six mugs of coffee, or 0.137 kilowatt hours per cup of coffee.

Boiling the kettle, however, takes only one minute 20 seconds and uses 2.74 kilowatts during that time, so each boil of the kettle uses 0.076 kilowatt hours. Six boils of the kettle would use 0.456 kilowatt hours.

Now I have the answer: the kettle is more environmentally friendly than the coffee maker at least in terms of electricity usage. (Unless of course I drank six mugs of coffee in less than an hour and a half, in which case I suspect my carbon emissions would be the least of my problems.) Of course this means I won't be able to feel good about putting coffee grounds in the compost bin.

CHAPTER 7

Month seven

"Because it's not stocked in supermarkets and if it was it would be relabelled as a speciality product and the price increased."

A common reason for not buying local produce.

As spring is quickly approaching, it is time to get to grips with the garden. My contribution to the destruction of the planet from working in the garden is probably negligible, but it does involve petrol driven lawnmowers, hedge trimmers and strimmers as well as burning a lot of garden waste. I should say that given a choice between bugs and pesticide residue I have always chosen pesticide residue as the lesser of two evils. This year however, I will try to be greener about it. But, as with all my green activities, it is worth thinking about what being green in the garden actually means for me, and how I can be greener without making the garden a less enjoyable part of the house.

There seem to be several areas where I can be greener in the garden, including:

1 Reducing (or even eliminating) the amounts of pesticide I spray, pour, and otherwise inflict on the natural environment

2 Not using garden products that have somehow damaged the environment in their production. (Peat based products are the main ones that spring to mind)

3 Making sure the garden is an environment that encourages wildlife

4 Using the garden to grow fruit and vegetables

We're not all that bad as it happens, and the garden is certainly a haven for wildlife. In the last few weeks alone we have had all the usual suspects, plus a couple of owls, a hummingbird hawk moth, and several dozen mice. In the case of the mice however, the majority of them have been consumed by the cats, which strikes me as the natural order of things, and even if it isn't, is certainly my preferred approach to rodents in the garden. There are bats in the attic, newts in the disused well, and frogs and toads in the compost heap. We're practically a site of special scientific interest, but I have no doubt we can do better.

I think the best thing though is to make the most use of the garden to produce things that we can eat, and then to make sure we use them. As usual there are trade offs to be made when gardening. It is clearly possible to garden without being green about it, and pesticides, chemical fertilisers and the like all take away from the green nature of gardening.

Certainly, in my pre-green existence I have not been averse to spraying everything in sight with whatever bottle of chemicals will promise to remove the most pests. Living next to a farm, we also have a regular problem with the number of flies that are produced, so managing these is a must, if we are to be able to use the garden at any time other than when it is raining.

There is a small greenhouse, and an equally small vegetable plot, but enough to keep the family in cucumbers and tomatoes for the summer months, thus destroying the Spanish agricultural economy at a stroke. Growing your own food is probably one of the most satisfying green activities it is possible to undertake, especially as (for a change) it doesn't involve giving anything up, cutting back, or generally feeling guilty about things.

Pest control however is the big issue. The mice are under control, thanks to the cats, but the flies need something to keep the numbers down. In the past I have bought a 'Red Top Fly Trap' whose advertising promises that "eighteen billion flies can't be wrong". It uses a bait that is particularly attractive to female flies and lures them into the trap where, sadly, they die. It is non-toxic, safe (as long as you're not a fly obviously) and each trap will collect something like 20,000 flies. The only downside is that the bait smells as if there's a dead animal lying out in the sun, but it's not normally noticeable unless I'm within about two feet of the trap. Within hours, these traps are working and clear almost the whole garden of any flies. As far as I can tell, this is far more effective than spraying insecticide on a weekly basis. It is nice when a more environmentally friendly option is also more effective at getting the job done.

CHAPTER 8

Month eight

"My daughter to be kidnapped by aliens."

One man's description of what would be needed to reduce his use
of the car.

There is news that a biodegradable bottle has now been launched by a mineral water company. This bottle can be thrown in the compost bin and will be soil in twelve weeks. This is somewhat faster than grapefruit peel, which strikes me as remarkable in itself.

I suppose that this is good news but, in a strange twist of logic, it seems to make my attempts at going green somewhat more irrelevant than ever.

There are two reasons for this.

Firstly, the development of biodegradable food packaging seems to lend weight to the argument that recycling is probably a waste of time as it is mankind's capacity for innovation that will save the planet rather than any attempt to adopt a more environmentally friendly lifestyle.

Secondly it adds more weight to the argument that the biggest changes to be made to the way in which our lifestyle impacts the environment can be made in the production of goods and services rather than in their consumption. One drinks company adopting a biodegradable bottle for distribution will undoubtedly have a more positive impact on the environment than thousands of consumers conscientiously putting their plastics out for the recycling truck.

The reason why this biodegradable food packaging has suddenly become viable seems to be a direct response to huge increases in the price of plastic packaging as a result of the increases in oil prices. This seems to suggest that relying on the market to develop solutions to environmental issues may be a credible solution. Again, I find this surprisingly depressing, as it supports an assumption that significant intervention in the market may not be necessary, so we can all go on buying whatever we want until eventually it is priced to a level where an environmentally friendly substitute becomes economically viable. Perhaps I should be pleased that as consumers we can save the planet by doing absolutely nothing.

I have to be honest that as time goes by we are slipping back into some of the old habits. The shopping bill seems to have risen inexorably not only back to its previous level but beyond. The biggest expense in the shopping bill (apart from what we shall euphemistically refer to as 'drinks') is definitely still meat. I do accept the argument that eating meat is a waste of resources due to the amount of land it takes to feed an animal, and the relative amount of food that could be produced from that land as a vegetarian choice versus the amount of food available from the animal itself. I just don't accept it enough to change my eating habits significantly, and despite foot and mouth, salmonella, mad cow, bird flu, e-coli outbreaks and all the rest of it, for some reason I have enough faith in the food chain to believe that it is safe. However, the more I think about it, the less faith I have.

I am sure it is time to reduce the amount of meat we consume as a family. This is more about health and cost than it is about the relative environmental benefits of vegetables or animals, or even the rights and wrongs of eating meat. (I happen to believe we're omnivores and that's it.) However, it would clearly be environmentally beneficial to discourage any growth in the number of cows in the world.

In response to this, I have decided we will start off with at least one vegetarian meal a week. The simple immediate options for this are pasta and pizza, both of which are just as good without any meat in them. Or so I believed. Dinner time is punctuated with screams of "but there's no pepperoni" as the kids notice the slightest variation from our usual pizza meal.

I am now wary that adapting a meal that we're used to eating with meat may not get past the kids, so my next attempt is to do stuffed peppers. This is a meal we have never had before. Neither of the kids eats any of it. It strikes me there is little environmental benefit to be achieved by throwing away cooked vegetables but I shall persevere.

To be honest, there are several areas where I am getting less enthusiastic about some of the green measures that we have adopted, particularly around the shopping. It was impossible to sustain using the small independent shops in the town for whatever I could buy there and using the supermarket for anything else. The supermarket is open 24 hours a day for six days a week and most of the day on the seventh. It almost always has everything in stock; it's easy to park; it's cheaper; someone will pack the bags if I want them to; and it doesn't involve dodging the traffic in the centre of town with two kids in tow.

The trouble is that once I'm in the supermarket, suddenly none of it matters. I am a supermarket shopper. The packaging, the food miles, the processed foods are all a part of the experience that somehow I should savour and enjoy. I still can't bring myself to buy organic food, simply because of the price, but non-organic seems more in keeping with the experience anyway.

CHAPTER 9

Month nine

"I live in the Midlands. We've got no shortage of water here."

So far, water hasn't been a big issue in my attempt to lead a greener lifestyle, and I have to admit it's hard to take water conservation seriously when I drive past three leaks in the mains on the school run in the morning that show no sign of ever being fixed. There is also the fact that (and whisper this quietly) we're not on a meter, so there's not all that much self-interest involved in saving water. However, given that we seem to be verging on permanent drought conditions (at least as far as the water companies are concerned, which isn't a huge surprise when they're covering the A422 in water for 24 hours a day) it feels as if I should do my bit.

I suspect we're as profligate with water as we are with anything else, although a quick review suggests we're not too bad in some areas.

1 We don't have a sprinkler system which can use 540 litres an hour

2 We don't have a swimming pool

3   We take showers rather than baths. A bath uses some 80 litres of water, while a five minute shower uses 35 litres

4   We have three water butts that collect water that is used for the garden

5   We have no dripping taps, which can use 140 litres of water a week

6   Using the dishwasher uses somewhere around 12-16 litres of water, while hand washing a full dishwasher load would use about 40 litres[34]

7   I have two kids who are seemingly incapable of flushing the toilet

These water statistics for an average household are quite frightening. We use 155 litres a day per person in the UK. A third of all household water is used to flush the toilet[35].

Most of the actions required to improve water usage seem to be relatively simple:

1   Turn the tap off while brushing our teeth. Cleaning teeth with the tap off will use about a litre of water, while leaving the tap running for a regulation five minute brushing twice a day would mean 240 litres a day in our house

2   Only use the dishwasher and the washing machine when there is a full load. A full load of washing uses less than twice the water of two half loads

3   Put any one of a range of water saving devices in the toilet cisterns. The most common seems to be the 'water-hippo'

from **www.hippo4life.co.uk**. These water displacement devices are available free of charge from some of the local water companies. In our case it seems we can have a 'Freddie Frog' for free, which beats paying for a water hippo. I have ordered two

It is obviously possible to go a lot further than this and install a complete system for reusing both grey water (water from the bath and such like that could be used for toilet flushing, where drinking quality water is not required – except for our cats who have the disgusting habit of drinking from the toilet bowl) or a rainwater system that collects water from the roof of the house and stores it for use in the house. None of these makes financial sense for us as there is no possible benefit to installing them while our water supply isn't metered, but it would be possible to reduce our use of what is a precious and frequently wasted resource, by just treating it with the respect it deserves.

In only a week, two of the three water leaks on the school run have been fixed which has done a lot to improve my motivation on water conservation. Freddie Frog has also turned up in the post. Disappointingly he isn't a frog at all, but is in fact just a half-litre plastic container with a screw on lid; the kind of thing that PVA glue normally comes in. I was hoping for something shaped like a frog that I could show to friends when they came to visit, and could use to convince the kids we had frogs living in the toilet cisterns. Maybe I should have gone for the hippo after all.

With summer approaching, the issue of water looms larger than at other times of the year. Summer also brings some other changes to the ease with which it is possible to be green.

1 The smell of the kitchen waste waiting to be put in the compost bin is stronger every day in the heat of summer

2 The pile of cardboard is growing every day as we're not using the fires as much. Some of this is now being composted along with the kitchen waste, but I suspect that if I tried to compost all of the cardboard we have in the house it would disturb the delicate balance of my composting mixture. Actually it would result in everything being completely overwhelmed by cardboard

However, summer also brings some benefits in that:

● We can dry all the clothes outside

● We aren't using the heating or the lighting as much

● More local produce is available in the supermarket (well, national produce anyway)

● The vegetable patch is showing signs of life with courgettes, radishes, rhubarb, green beans, carrots and onions, and cucumbers and tomatoes in the greenhouse

All in all, it seems much easier to be green during the summer months, apart from the undeniable temptation to buy a cheap air conditioning unit.

CHAPTER 10

Month ten

"And as for supermarkets with unrecyclable packaging.
Aaaaaargggh."

It is my father's birthday soon, and I will have to get him a gift. As with all fathers he is particularly difficult to buy for, unless I fall back on the standard shirt, socks and handkerchief options. As it is a landmark birthday for him, none of these options seem to be appropriate. Unfortunately this doesn't alter the fact that he is difficult to buy for. In line with my new lifestyle I am going to buy a green gift.

The options are remarkable. I could get him an acre of rainforest from **www.worldlandtrust.org**. This sounds like a wonderful gift, but I am worried about how I'm going to wrap it. We could get a tree from **www.tree2mydoor.com** or, staying with the tree theme I could buy a tree in a celebrity forest from **www.carbonneutral.com**. Unfortunately, the process of making a choice between David Gray's forest and Atomic Kitten's is proving too difficult for me. It is also possible to buy a carbon offset for a car for a year. These are available from the Go Green Foundation (**www.faithfulfish.co.uk**) who will happily sell a carbon offset package that includes:

- A GoGreen window badge for the window of your car that shows that you are making a difference & taking responsibility for the environment

- A certificate from The Carbon Neutral Company showing the dedication of 1 tree, offset produced, and a map of the forest where your tree is planted. All presented in cream folder, tied with ribbon

- A 'recycle your phone' bag[36]

I have to admit I'm not convinced. For me, making a guilt payment to someone feels like a poor substitute for actually reducing my impact on the environment. If I want to plant a tree then I'll put one in the garden and get the benefit of looking at it as well as offsetting some carbon emissions. The cream folder tied with ribbon is tempting though.

To be fair, much of the money is also used for promoting green energy use and providing grants for people who want to change their car or home to be more energy efficient, although why anyone who can afford to buy a new hybrid car would need a grant to do so is beyond me.

There is a huge number of environmentally friendly gifts that are available, from solar powered mobile phone chargers, and wind up radios, to fair trade chocolates, and recycled gifts, but in this case I want to buy something that is a contribution to the planet rather than a use of resources. Of course with any physical item that I buy there are a number of questions that have to be asked to establish if it is truly an environmentally friendly gift. Where was it made? How far was it transported in order to get to me? How was it made? What were the carbon emissions during manufacture? Was child labour involved in its manufacture? It is eminently possible that the solar powered environmentally friendly gift was made in a sweat shop somewhere that caused huge environmental damage in its manufacture and then travelled thousands of miles in order to get to me. These are just some of the things they don't put in the brochure.

As a result, I have finally decided to adopt a turtle from the Marine Conservation Society at **www.mcsuk.org**. I have been assured I won't need to wrap it. am now waiting to hear on the news that a rampaging gang of adopted turtles is destroying all marine life in the Pacific, but maybe I'm just becoming more cynical.

The more I think about them, the more I am taken by the idea of green gifts. I have decided that two nieces who have birthdays coming up should also be the proud recipients of adopted animals. Options include a king penguin on the Falkland Islands from **www.falklandsconservation.com** or a poison frog at Whipsnade Wild Animal Park from **www.zsl.org**. I think they may prefer a penguin.

To my immense surprise, these gifts have been better received than anything else we have bought in recent years. The two nieces are delighted with their penguins (now named Waddle and Sammy) and my father is pleased with the turtle as well, but has refrained from naming it.

CHAPTER 11

Month eleven

The summer is proving to be much easier in terms of living a greener life. At home, the lights are not on as much, the heating isn't on and the kids are spending more time wrecking the garden than they are sitting in front of the television. In the shops it is easier to buy locally produced fresh food, and drinking more cold drinks and less tea and coffee means the kettle isn't permanently on. The only blot on this horizon is when I wander round the DIY warehouse store and see row upon row of air conditioning machines available for less than the price of a decent fridge, and with the potential to consume more power in the summer than the heating does in the winter. It is hard to believe that there is such a great need for air conditioning units in the UK. When it's 104 in the shade day after day then I can see why it might be useful, but unless there are some predictions for this summer that I have missed, then I am not sure these represent a useful addition to our electricity bill.

A strange thing is beginning to happen to me though. I am becoming a bit of a green anorak. I honestly didn't expect this to happen. I am becoming increasingly frustrated by the facts that:

- I really don't think my own actions will have the slightest impact on the environment

- It is increasingly difficult to justify taking a lot of green actions due to the cost. Why pay five times as much for an organic T shirt when you can buy a perfectly good non-organic one?

- Huge changes could be achieved in how environmentally friendly my lifestyle is if those changes were made to the production and distribution of goods, and the environmental costs were reflected in the cost of goods and services to the consumer

- We have a society and a system in which it is incredibly difficult to be green. Our nearest shop is six miles away, the nearest pub four miles; the bus runs once a week; it isn't safe to send the kids off to school on their own; non-organic food is cheap, even if it's been flown in from Africa

So, on the basis that it isn't worth it, it isn't really my fault, and the very fact of existence in our society implies a level of environmental impact, in terms of saving the planet going green would seem to be a waste of effort unless everyone does it.

On the other hand, the process of trying to be greener is becoming easier, and more interesting as time goes by. I can understand how people become obsessed with it. The more I try to avoid environmental damage, the more annoyed I get when I discover something else I do that causes environmental damage, and then the more determined I am to stop that particular activity, and so on, in what could be a virtuous circle of continuously reducing environmental impact. I would never have thought that washing up a yoghurt pot could have such a long lasting effect on me.

Increasingly I am sure that the answer to being greener comes from making it easier for people. For example, the survey for this book showed a very high level of recycling by people, in particular when there was a doorstep collection available or easy access to a recycling centre.

- If you take plastics for example, 58% of people recycled their plastics through a doorstep collection by the local authority. Where there was no doorstep collection 55% put plastic in the general rubbish, while 45% took it to a recycling centre

- Where recycling points are less easily available and there is no doorstep collection the numbers fall dramatically, with only 16% claiming they recycled paint, and most admitting to leaving old paint in the shed until it dried up and then putting it out for the rubbish

- Only 30% claimed to recycle batteries, with most of the rest putting them out in general rubbish, with the exception of those like me who now have a box of old batteries in the garage (along with the paint)

Some of it may also be just down to habit as well as the easy availability of recycling points. So for example, only 1% of respondents put glass in the rubbish, with 53% recycling through doorstep collection, and 46% taking bottles to a recycling point.

For green waste 49% were composting it, while 22% had a doorstep recycling collection. 21% were putting it in general rubbish, with only 8% taking it to a recycling point. I suspect that much of this may be down to a reluctance to travel very far with a bag of rotting vegetation in the car.

However, at this point of the year, I am starting to see some of the benefits of having a bit more focus on the green nature of life. The cherry tree in the garden has just delivered about seven pounds of cherries, some of which are even edible. The apple trees are loaded with apples that are due in a couple of months, and the pear tree has yet to be completely eaten by wasps.

We are using compost that has been made from vegetation that would normally have found its way to a landfill site somehow (and has also saved me from making a trip to the garden centre to buy some). We have succeeded in trading excess cherries with a neighbour, in return for which we have raspberries and lettuces.

About the only major problem is that there is no longer a need for a fire to keep the house warm, so we are amassing cardboard in the garage and the shed faster than I can do anything with it. I am composting some of it, but if it all went in the compost bin I suspect it would not be long before I just had a container of wet cardboard rotting away in the garden. I am somehow resisting the temptation just to have a big bonfire.

CHAPTER 12

Month twelve

This is the final month of the experiment in trying to be more environmentally friendly in the way we live. I admit that it has probably been close to an exercise in trying to be less environmentally damaging in the way we live, but that all depends on how you look at it.

What has been interesting is how much more environmentally friendly we can be without really sacrificing anything very much, but by just being smarter about the way we do things and considering the impact of our own actions. This would seem to me to be the best way to try and go about improving things. If there is a need for a full scale lifestyle change by the majority of the population then that just isn't going to happen any time soon, but if small incremental changes can eventually create a real change then that is more likely to be accepted and successful.

In some ways I am embarrassed by what we were like at the beginning of this project. There was really no reasonable excuse for wasting the amount of electricity we were or for recycling as little as we did.

However, month 12 has seen the final attack on the electricity use in the house. Armed with my electrisave device I have finally got to the point where I can actually feel as if we have at least reached the point where we are no longer using more electricity than the average home in the UK. This may not sound like much of an achievement, but from a starting point of more than 40 kilowatt hours per day, to be able even to see 14 feels like a miracle.

There are two factors that drive our use above the average:

- We both work at home and so the house is occupied all day with the constant use of office equipment

- We are not connected to mains sewage, so there is a sewage treatment system that requires a pump to run for 24 hours a day

Home working costs us about five kilowatt hours per day, and the sewage treatment system costs six kilowatt hours per day. (I could turn the sewage treatment plant off, but that's not going to improve the environment, believe me.) With average usage, our house should use something in the order of 25 kilowatt hours per day. For this month, we have ranged between 22 and 26 kilowatt hours per day, with an average of just under 24, so if I take off the effects of home working and the sewage treatment pump, our electricity usage is now running at 13 kilowatt hours per day. On a like for like comparison this is down by 22 kilowatt hours per day from when we started this exercise.

A lot of things have become habit, and not only for me, but for the whole family. The kids know what goes in recycling and they at least ask whether clothes should go in the washing pile rather than assume that they should just because they've been worn for 20 minutes. Occasionally they even switch the lights off. Our weekly shopping has drifted away from the heady days when we cut the shopping bill in half but it is still less than it was by changing what we buy to avoid the expensive and over packaged items on the shelves.

However, the fact that the shopping has drifted back to closer to where it used to be is an indication of how easy it is to stop being greener if I don't think about it. Daily life is full of non-green options, most of which seem to be the easy option at the time. It is easier to make a special trip to do the shopping without the kids in tow rather than combine it with the school run; it is easier to buy a packaged pizza than it is to make one from scratch; it is easier to buy prepackaged vegetables than it is to buy them loose; it is easier to go to bed with the television on standby than it is to remember to turn it off, and it is certainly easier to put the clothes in the wash pile than it is to fold them up and put them away.

Although many of the changes have become habit, it is very easy to slip back into the old ways out of sheer laziness. Fortunately it is the time of year when it seems easier to be green. The days are longer; the sun is shining; and right now, the garden is producing cucumbers, tomatoes and blackcurrants in abundance.

Once again, there is an irony in that although producing some of our own food on however limited a scale is a green option, the fact that it all comes at the same time immediately incurs an environmental cost in terms of filling a freezer with things from the garden, and running the cooker to make jams, chutneys and the like. We will have the same problem with apples which will have to be made into pies and apple sauce, blackberries which will have to be made into jams and pies, and figs, which none of us like, so they will all be given to a neighbour. However, there is something about eating things from the garden that is extremely satisfying, even if it is not completely without a cost.

It is this time of year when I can understand how some people think that some form of self-sufficiency is the answer to being green. I think once again it is one of those things where it is unfortunate that this confusion exists as it makes green living seem once again as if it involves getting up at five in the morning to milk the goat, and toiling in the fields like some sort of mediaeval tithed peasant farmer until it is time to fall exhausted into bed. It just puts me off the whole idea.

I did, however, in this last month of trying to be greener, finally lose patience with the supermarket. My early enquiry as to whether they would stock more environmentally friendly cleaning products was responded to with what I guess is standard answer number 47 which went along the lines of 'we stock our stores in line with customer demand, and as demand changes, yahdi yahdu yah'. So I have been to the local health food store, where they stock all the environmentally friendly stuff, along with lots of other very odd things as well and we now have environmentally friendly dishwasher tablets, rinsing agent, washing powder, bathroom cleaner: the lot. So, let's hope the supermarket notes that down as a change in customer demand.

Strangely, there is also news that the hole in the ozone layer is closing. Could my efforts over the last year really have had such a positive effect? I doubt it. This news about the ozone layer feels strange. Long before anyone had really heard of greenhouse gases or global warming, it was the hole in the ozone layer that was the most likely cause of climatic chaos, and increased sales of factor 60 sun cream. If the hole in the ozone layer can start to close, then perhaps there is hope after all.

On a final positive note, this was also the month when my youngest child finally gave up her use of disposable nappies. This has reduced both the shopping bill and the contents of the wheelie bin significantly. I am now totally in favour of reusable nappies, and strongly believe that everyone should be made to use them rather than disposables.

CHAPTER 13

Did it do any good?

The big question at the end of this time trying to go green without going mad about it, is whether it has all been worth it. Have we saved the planet? Probably not. Have we personally reduced our greenhouse gas emissions? Certainly. We have driven fewer miles, used less petrol, used less electricity and used less heating oil. Specifically:

- Compared with the previous 12 months we have reduced our electricity consumption by 27%

- We have reduced our petrol consumption for the 4x4 by 48%

- We have reduced our rubbish by about 60%, although I do now have a box of old batteries and a vast collection of cardboard in the garage

- We have reduced our consumption of plastic bags by 90 per cent. (I still forget to take the reusable bags once in a while)

- Our oil consumption for central heating has reduced by about 10%

There have been a lot of surprises along the way.

Just how much electricity we wasted by not even using it was an incredible shock. It wasn't even just profligacy; it was sheer waste to have devices consuming power when we weren't using them. Over the time of this diary, our electricity usage has nearly halved, and we didn't do anything particularly special to achieve that.

Month	Kilowatt hours	Average Kilowatt hours per day
September	1,380	46
October	1,230	40
November	1,028	34
December	971	31
January	1,004	32
February	810	29
March	941	30
April	574	19
May	811	26
June	744	25
July	786	25
August	702	23

- September represents our pre-green usage of electricity
- The particularly low usage in April is due to a two week

family vacation, thus disproving the belief that there is no environmental benefit to be achieved by flying to the USA

At the reduced level of electricity usage that we have achieved, the vast majority of this is used whether anyone is in the house or not. This seems to be purely the result of old domestic appliances that it does not make financial sense to change. I also suspect that the environmental benefits of continuing to use an old appliance, rather than incurring the environmental costs of manufacturing a new one, means that however bad these appliances are, they are better than buying new ones when there is still life left in the old appliances. In particular, more than half of our base level electrical usage can be put down to the freezer and the pump on the sewage treatment unit that we have as a result of not being connected to the main drainage system.

In terms of incremental usage that we can manage by turning things off when they're not in use: that has reduced by 83%. Our overall usage has reduced by 46%. Although some of this change is seasonal due to the timing of this green diary, the year on year reduction has been 27%.

The amount of food we throw away has also been a huge shock. Once I was separating out food waste that could go into the compost bin it suddenly became clear how much was being thrown away. Ironically most of this food had also travelled many thousands of miles just to become compost in the garden. Shrivelled, uneaten grapes, black bananas beyond even the last resort of banana bread, celery hidden at the bottom of the salad drawer in the fridge for weeks on end are all in the compost. It is irritating that we paid for this food and then threw it out without eating it. I am now absolutely certain that if the whole population only bought what they actually ate, the supermarkets would all be struggling to survive within a week. As a nation, about 20% of the food we buy each year is thrown into the bin. This equates to about £424 of food thrown away every year by every household[37].

And that's another (and unwelcome) side effect of trying to be greener. I have become increasingly irritated with an ever growing number of facets of daily life that used to just wash over me. Food on the supermarket shelf that's right at the use by date, local produce that looks as if it had to walk down the hard shoulder of the M1 in order to get to the supermarket, while produce that flew intercontinental looks as if it did it first class with an eye mask and hot and cold running stewardesses to look after it. How English apples can be bruised, battered and generally unappealing, while anything from New Zealand can manage to look fresh and inviting, is something of a conundrum.

And I'm increasingly annoyed with my fellow citizens. When I take the kids to school and I drive past the rows of houses close to the school and see the overflowing wheelie bins with the supplementary black bags and one or two cardboard boxes that had contained the plasma television for the spare bedroom, I get annoyed. I want to knock on every door and get them to explain to me just why they think they're entitled to such excess, when every other programme on their new television is about how much of a mess the planet is in. Which part of their brain couldn't make the connection between their own rubbish and the pictures of the mountains of waste that the country no longer seems to have the capability to deal with?

I have become less tolerant of those who don't make an effort. This may not be pleasant, but I am telling myself that it is better than being one of the smug self-righteous greens who are already starting to say 'I told you so'. Ironically I have also become less tolerant of those who make too much of an effort. For some reason, a lot of people seem to have gone out of their way to make being green too damn difficult for most of the population, thereby leaving us mere mortals with a choice between living in a state of perpetual worry and guilt, or choosing to ignore the issue completely. Unfortunately, most of us have chosen to ignore the issue completely. Life's too short, and there are more immediate things to worry about than whether Norfolk's going to be a bit wetter than normal by the end of the century. It seems that for some people you can only be green if you never travel by air, don't own a car, don't have a life, and only eat what you can dig out of the dumpsters behind the supermarket. If that's how they want to live their life, good luck to them, but it's not for me, and I refuse to believe that they have got it right. If that is the lifestyle we need to adopt in order to save the planet then, frankly, they can forget it because normal folk just aren't going to do it.

I have also become less tolerant of the scientists associated with the whole green debate. I am in the fortunate position of being unencumbered by knowledge as far as the science of climate change goes, but even to me it all looks dubious. Firstly, let's remember that this is a science roughly based on weather forecasting. Given that current weather forecasting technology seems unable to produce a forecast that remains the same for more than a few hours, and is then almost unerringly inaccurate, why we should believe that we can forecast anything 100 years from now is frankly asking too much.

Watching the television recently, I was struck by the apparent dishonesty of the climate debate. I am guessing that it is an attempt to make a complex subject understandable, but too much of the time seems to be spent presenting hypotheses as hard facts, and making huge leaps of logic that are justified by inserting the word 'could' as in 'these significant changes in weather patterns could be evidence of global warming'. What they want to say is 'changes in the weather are evidence of global warming', even though they can't prove that. By inserting the word 'could' then suddenly everyone is being honest. What they might just as easily be saying is 'the changing weather patterns could have no connection whatsoever with global warming'. There is too much politics and spin becoming associated with the issue.

Another of the negatives about this whole process is that it has turned me into even more of an eco-worrier. It's not as if I didn't have enough things to worry about, but now going green has added another one. I notice when something is on the television, and I read the articles when I see them in the newspaper. (As an aside, I suspect we could significantly reduce the carbon emissions that are causing climate change if we stopped sending camera crews to the Arctic Circle to report on the impacts of climate change.)

Finally, after changing the way in which we do things in order to try and live a greener lifestyle, I have revisited the carbon footprint calculators that shocked me at the beginning of this little adventure.

Some of the sites that I originally used to try and find one that didn't make me feel awful about what I was doing have since disappeared, but as a comparison:

- The BP carbon footprint calculator now thinks I am emitting eight tonnes of carbon dioxide per annum. This is compared with its original estimate of twenty four tonnes. So a reduction of 67%

- Before I get too carried away, the Earthday ecological footprint calculator tells me that I still need 5.5 hectares of land to support my lifestyle, or 3.1 planets. This means I have saved 2.1 planets since the initial evaluation. This sounds a lot better than the fact that I am still using 3.1

- Carbonfootprint.com now tells me that I am emitting 13,943 kg of CO_2 compared with a UK average of 10,963 kg. Originally I was using 36,825 kg per annum, so again this is a reduction of about 62%

- Climatestar now suspects that I am emitting 11.17 tonnes of CO_2 per annum, compared with a pre-green estimate of 36.92 tonnes per annum. Again this is a reduction of 70%

- The Conservation Fund still thinks I am emitting 22 tonnes of carbon dioxide a year, but as this is a site which allows me to make a donation to offset my carbon emissions at a click of a mouse, I am not that surprised

Now, while I admit that this is probably an improvement from being incredibly environmentally unfriendly to just being vaguely environmentally unfriendly, this is still quite a positive change, and the only way I am ever going to use less than 3.1 planets seems to be by becoming a vegetarian, which isn't going to happen.

However, the important question is whether it actually cost me any more money by trying to live a greener life. I admit to not buying organic food as that would have negated any saving I did make, but I estimate that:

- Savings on the car in the year were approximately £600

- The reduced cost of the weekly shopping saved approximately £800

- The reduced electricity bills saved about £315

- Savings on purchase of bags of compost for the garden £15

Additional costs were minimal.

- Replacement of strip plugs £60.00

- Electrisave monitor £75.00

- Compost Bins £10.00

All this gave a net saving from trying to be greener of £1,585 which is nearly enough for an organic cabbage.

Perhaps more importantly, however, this last year has changed the way I think about what I am doing on a daily basis. I do now consider the environmental impact of my actions, but without worrying too much about it. I have come to terms with the fact that anything I do has some sort of impact. The key thing is to make the choice that I believe has the least impact. Our life doesn't feel very different, probably because so much of what needs to be done is simple to do, easily becomes a habit and fits into the day without being a special effort.

However, there is no doubt that I could do more. The issue, more than anything, is one of convenience. If the UK is to be green, then green needs to be the easy and the default choice for any action. Specifically:

- There needs to be a greater level of doorstep collection of recyclable waste, especially plastics, green waste, and cardboard

- All packaging should be recyclable. According to DEFRA, 40% of all waste in bins is retail packaging. That is outrageous

- There should be greater availability of local produce in supermarkets. If they can all have an organic section I'm not sure what is stopping them having a local section as well

- Plastic bags should be charged for (as they already are in many European countries)

But, sadly, not everything can be done by someone else. Some of it involves a conscious lifestyle change, for example:

- We need to change the way we eat in order to eat more local (and therefore almost inevitably seasonal) produce. Lettuce in January is never going to be a good idea

- We need to think twice before getting in the car

It is also inevitable that there are people who, whatever opportunity they are given to live a greener lifestyle, are not going to take it. There is (and it really does hurt me to say this) almost no way out of admitting the inevitability that there will need to be greater incentives for people to be green. This will almost certainly be greater economic disincentives to be a muddy brown through higher energy costs, direct charging for waste disposal, higher taxes on environmentally unfriendly vehicles, enforced water metering, and the like. There is little doubt in my mind that being environmentally unfriendly is going to get a lot more expensive in the future, especially as it provides such a good excuse for another new tax to be imposed. Proposals are already on the table for us all to have our own individual carbon allowance that we will then have to live within, or pay to buy additional allowances.

There is one element of all of this greenness that I find considerably confusing; actually, more than one, but one in particular. If the threat of global climate change is the biggest threat facing mankind today, then why isn't anybody really doing anything about it?

It's all very well having recycling campaigns, turning down our thermostats by one degree and buying organic chocolate when the fancy takes us, but I can't help thinking that it's going to need more than that if the problem is as big as is suggested.

Our response seems very half-hearted from the governmental institutions, and any real action seems to have been left to an eclectic collection of single issue pressure groups who seem to address things with an endearing level of amateurish enthusiasm, but without any real power to do anything. Those who have the power to do something seem reluctant to do anything.

Some simple questions:

- Why are the supermarkets still allowed to give away free plastic bags?

- Why are electronic devices even allowed to have a standby option?

- Why is it permissible to manufacture anything other than energy efficient devices?

- Why is the tax from fuel not being used to offset carbon emissions?

- Why is energy from renewables being so inadequately developed?

- Why are local authorities being allowed to start incinerating things just to avoid landfill?

- Why are local authorities not obliged to collect all recyclable materials?

- Why do we offer subsidies for bizarrely expensive solar panels for domestic use when the money could almost certainly be better spent elsewhere?

- Why are so many people not even aware they could buy energy from renewable sources?

If ever there was a case for mandating action, this would be it. A situation where everyone's individual actions have little or no impact, but the combined environmental abuse being perpetrated by most of us could be the catalyst for some sort of environmental apocalypse.

Not enough people will make the effort when their neighbours aren't. It will be some time before a full wheelie bin will generate the level of moral outrage that will make people change their habits. Trying to change the habits and attitudes of 60 million people seems as if it would be more difficult than mandating action by a much smaller number of manufacturers and governmental institutions.

If this is the world's biggest issue, it is a sad reflection on us all that it is being addressed in such a shambolic and ineffective way. It is also probably the case that the environmental calamity we are supposed to be facing isn't just an issue of lifestyle. It is also an issue of the sheer number of people in the world. The combination of increasing levels of individual consumption and a growing global population is an environmental double whammy for which there does not seem to be adequate action being taken. I can imagine that future generations (should they be fortunate enough to exist) will look back on the environmental actions of this time in the same way that we now watch 'Duck and Cover' information films on how to survive a nuclear attack by crawling under the desk. Hopefully they will have the chance to find us equally amusing, if a little quaint and naive.

Afterword

Just in case you're wondering. Yes, I will be keeping up the greener lifestyle even though I won't be keeping a diary any more. No, I didn't lose any weight or feel particularly healthier as a result. I did save some money though, and my eco-guilt level has significantly reduced. I don't really consider myself to be a reluctant green any more either. I'm seriously considering growing a beard and wearing hemp sandals. Well, maybe not.

I'm now an irritated green. Irritated that it remains so difficult to make the green choice and irritated by those who don't seem to realise that.

Appendix – Some hints and tips

There are some aspects of being greener that are easier than others, mainly just due to the convenience of the green option rather than any huge issue about how difficult it is to do. There are ways to make it easier.

1 Starting the process in late spring or early summer helps in a number of ways:

   - Firstly, the days are getting longer, so the electricity bills go down because there is less need to have the lights on

   - More local produce is available, which makes it easier to cut down on the food miles of the weekly shop

   - It is easier to get clothes drying outside in the summer

   - There is less heating expense in the summer

2 Involving the whole family in the exercise is the only option. It's bad enough going round cleaning up after kids all day without also having to take the recycling out of the rubbish bin. Introduce the kids to the concept of putting clean clothes away in the cupboard rather than in the washing pile

3 Keep a record of things like electricity usage and the

amount of rubbish you throw out. It is useful to be able to remind yourself of how much things have improved whenever it feels like it's all too much trouble

4   Do whatever you can around the house to make it easy to switch things off by organising plugs and using strip plugs or multiway adapters with individual switches for each socket

5   Green the house room by room

IN THE KITCHEN

- Only put the amount of water you need in the kettle. (I always thought this was a really pathetic piece of advice, but it really works at reducing the electricity consumption)

- Use a microwave to reheat or warm food rather than the oven

- Close the fridge door (unless you're actually trying to get something out of the fridge)

- Put kitchen waste in a compost bin

- Have a meal plan and use it to determine what food you buy, rather than just buy stuff and then see what you can make with it. Only buy what you're going to eat

- Get a collection of recipes that use food that is past its best rather than throw it away. Personal favourites include banana bread, strawberry daiquiris, vegetable soup and bread and butter pudding

- Fill the freezer with something (scrunched up newspaper if necessary) as it uses less power than freezing air

- Compost cardboard packaging

IN THE UTILITY ROOM

- Only run the dishwasher on a full load

- Only run the washing machine on a full load

- Use a cold wash in the washing machine whenever possible

- Don't wash clean clothes

- Use environmentally friendly washing powders and dishwasher tablets

- Dry clothes outside or on an inside line rather than in a clothes dryer

IN THE LIVING ROOM

- Turn the television off rather than on to standby

- Ditto, the VCR, Digibox, DVD, stereo and all the rest of it

IN THE BATHROOM

- Have a shower rather than a bath

- Don't install a power shower

- Turn the tap off when cleaning your teeth

- Get a free water displacement device from your water company and put it in the toilet cistern

IN THE WHOLE HOUSE

- Turn the thermostat down by one degree

- Fit thermostatic valves on the radiators

- Fit electricity saving light bulbs

- Turn the lights off when you leave the room (unless there are other people in there)

- Organise plugs so that it is easier to switch things off at the wall socket

- Use strip plugs and multiway adapters with individual switches

- Switch to a green energy provider

- Sign up to the mailing preference service and reduce your junk mail

- Get bills online and reduce mail even further

- Recycle anything you can

- Fix any leaking taps

- Buy recycled products when you can (**www.recycledproducts.org.uk**)

IN THE STUDY

- Recycle the print cartridges from the printer or get them refilled

- Don't print everything. (A laser printer is second only to the kettle in terms of making the electricity meter speed up)

- Reuse paper for printing if possible

- Don't power up the printer unless you're going to use it

- Don't put your mobile phone on permanent recharge

IN THE GARAGE/WORKSHOP/SHED

- Turn off any power tools sitting on charge

- Recycle the paint and be amazed at how much more shelf space you have

IN THE GARDEN

- Don't use a sprinkler for the lawn

- Don't use peat based compost products

- Buy a compost bin (at a reduced price from local authority if you can) and use it for kitchen waste

- Use a non-toxic form of pest control

- Get a water butt and collect rainwater for the garden

- Have a vegetable patch

- Buy recycled garden furniture

AT THE SHOPS

- Try to buy food that has not travelled thousands of miles

- Try to buy food that isn't heavily packaged

- Buy fruit and vegetables loose rather than prepackaged

- Buy products in packaging that can be recycled and check this in the store

- Use reusable bags rather than plastic carrier bags

- Only buy the food you're going to eat (and leave the 20% we all throw away on the shelves)

- Try to use local shops when you can

Footnotes

[1] Source DEFRA **www.defra.gov.uk**

[2] For example, respondents were asked how many litres of water would be wasted if the tap was left running while they brushed their teeth for five minutes. The real answer is 30 litres, but anything between 15 and 45 was counted as within the margin of error.

[3] Source: Reported in The Sunday Times, 4th December 2005.

[4] Source: Reported on news.bbc.co.uk

[5] Climate Issues and Questions, George C Marshall Institute, 2004.

[6] The Guardian, 27th January 2005.

[7] I admit that as conspiracy theories go this isn't exactly Da Vinci caliber, but have you ever considered why cows do nothing but eat grass all day?.

[8] Source: **www.mpsonline.org**.

[9] Source: The National Energy Foundation **www.nef.org.uk**

[10] Source: "It's in the bag" a report by Best Foot Forward, www.bestfootforward.com.

[11] Source: **www.adoptabeach.org.uk**

[12] Source: Steel Recycling Information Bureau, **www.scrib.org**

[13] Source: **www.recyclenow.co.uk/index.php**

[14] Source: Women's Environmental Network **www.wen.org.uk/nappies/cost_comparison.htm**

[15] See *Full Time Father – How to Succeed as a Stay at Home Dad,* White Ladder Press, 2004.

[16] Lifecycle Assessment of Disposable and Reusable Nappies in the UK, The Environment Agency, May 2005.

[17] www.wen.org.uk/rnw/nappy_facts.htm

[18] www.thameswateruk.co.uk

[19] To be fair to tetrapak here, the cartons are recyclable 'where facilities exist' and the issue is that the council doesn't collect them.
Some local councils will collect tetrapak cartons. Details are available at **www.tetrapakrecycling.co.uk**. The innocent drinks company (those of the smoothies) is also running a letter writing campaign to try and get more councils to recycle tetrapak cartons. More details at **www.innocentdrinks.co.uk/recycle**. One can only wish them luck, and send a letter to the council. Of course, the fact that the main UK recycling plant for these containers shut down in June 2006 quite possibly means that this isn't going to do much good, but that's just another example of the many green ironies that seem to exist.

[20] Source: **www.envirogreen.co.uk**

[21] Source: **www.wasteonline.org.uk**

[22] **www.wasteonline.org.uk**

[23] DEFRA Report "The Validity of Food Miles as an Indicator of Sustainable Development" July 15th 2005

[24] Office for National Statistics: The Impact of UK Households on the Environment through Direct and Indirect Generation of Greenhouse Gases. October 2004.

[25] **www.mcsuk.org**

26 www.thealternativechristmaslist.co.uk

27 West Wales Eco Centre
www.ecocentre.org.uk/a-green-christmas.html

28 Source: Adapted from; Renewable Energy, Campaign for the Protection of Rural England.

29 Source: Royal Society for the Protection of Birds **www.rspb.org.uk**

30 Source:
www.defra.gov.uk/environment/statistics/waste/kf/wrkf02.htm

31 Source: The Zero Waste Alliance UK, **www.zwallianceuk.org**

32 Source: Department of Trade and Industry, UK Energy in Brief, July 2005.

33 Source: Energy Future **www.energyfuture.org.uk**

34 Source The Environment Agency **www.environment-agency.gov.uk**

35 Source Thames Water; **www.thames-water.com**

USEFUL LINKS

We've put together a list of useful organisations to contact if you want to get a bit greener, or at least find out more about it. As contact details often change we've put the list on our website where we can update it regularly, rather than printed it here. You can find the list at **www.whiteladderpress.com**; click on 'useful links' next to the information about this book.

If you don't have access to the Internet you can contact White Ladder Press by any of the means listed on the next page and we'll print off a hard copy and post it to you free of charge.

CONTACT US

You're welcome to contact White Ladder Press if you have any questions or comments for either us or the authors. Please use whichever of the following routes suits you.

Phone: 01803 813343

Email: enquiries@whiteladderpress.com

Fax: 01803 813928

Address: White Ladder Press, Great Ambrook, Near Ipplepen, Devon TQ12 5UL

Website: www.whiteladderpress.com

WHAT CAN OUR WEBSITE DO FOR YOU?

If you want more information about any of our books, you'll find it at **www.whiteladderpress.com**. In particular you'll find extracts from each of our books, and reviews of those that are already published. We also run special offers on future titles if you order online before publication. And you can request a copy of our free catalogue.

Many of our books have links pages, useful addresses and so on relevant to the subject of the book. You'll also find out a bit more about us and, if you're a writer yourself, you'll find our submission guidelines for authors. So please check us out and let us know if you have any comments, questions or suggestions.

Fancy another good read?

If you've enjoyed *Diary of a Reluctant Green* how about trying another of our books? If your local area is threatened by incursions from big business or government, and you want to campaign to protect it, take a look at *Not In Our Back Yard How to run a protest campaign and save the neighbourhood.* Written by Antony Jay, co-author of *Yes, Minister* and *Yes, Prime Minister,* this is an invaluable guide to everything you need to know. As Grand Designs magazine said, "Writing clearly and with a touch of humour, he manages to make the whole darned business both informative and entertaining. If you follow his advice to the letter your campaigns should have major repercussions. Those local councils had better watch their backs."

Here's a taster of what you'll find in *Not In Our Back Yard.* If you like the look of it and want to order a copy, you can call us on 01803 813343 or order online at **www.whiteladderpress.com**.

The Barrage

from part 3: The battle is joined

The barrage is chiefly an electronic and paper barrage, and most of this section is devoted to the loading, aiming and firing of emails and letters; but you will also have to use the telephone from time to time. You will do well to think of the telephone simply as a means of acquiring information; it is not as good as an email or letter for conducting arguments, extracting admissions or making representations, except in emergencies – for instance when you see through the window that the bulldozer driver is actually fastening the chain round the oak tree which is under a Tree Preservation Order. Most of your work will be done through junior officials at lower levels.

But it is letters (snail-mailed or emailed), not telephone calls, that carry the weight of the barrage. A large part of the campaign will be won or lost on paper, which is the chosen weapon of civilised government, and you can turn this to your advantage. A part of your objective has already been mentioned in the previous paragraph – the extraction of information and admissions which will be valuable to you later. The Experts' Cell must put in all the work they can, and they may be surprised by the discrepancies they reveal when they compare replies from different departments and branches of government. The replies may also give them useful leads by betraying homework not properly done before the plan was published. A really wide spread of correspondence will be a great help when mounting the counter-attack.

But there is another purpose to the barrage. A steady stream of sensible and critical emails and letters that demand careful replies has a powerful softening up effect. Officials will begin to realise that it is going to be a very tough campaign, giving them a lot of extra work and plenty of opportunities for slipping up or getting caught out. After all, they have plenty of work to do, without answering tricky correspondence, and if every member of the Experts' Cell is writing two or three emails or letters a week, the cumulative effect after a month will be noticeable.

The worst sort of email or letter, from your point of view, is one that takes you an hour to compose, and is answered in two minutes. Conversely, the message that you can dash off quickly, and that keeps the official busy for a long time concocting the answer, is what you are aiming for. Their standard response to a letter from the public is to be brief, non-committal and uninformative. If they can simply reply, '… will bear your views in mind…', or '… ensure that your remarks be brought to the attention of …', or '… information not at present available …', then they have won and you have lost. If you have an experienced and senior civil servant in one of your teams, they should look at all the early emails and letters and show the writers how they could have been improved, but the principle is straightforward enough: make sure your messages contain some suggestion that cannot be left unrefuted on the file. There are *seven main categories of allegation or implication* which sting them into activity.

Ignorance: if they have to admit you know more than they do, their credibility in defence of the plan will be seriously eroded. So you can keep them busy with questions like, 'Surely section 43 para vi of the plan conflicts with the principles stated in Mr Tashima's famous paper at Kyoto in 1997?' (A refinement is to give the wrong reference first time, so when they finally come up with that discovery you can say, 'I meant of course Mr Onishi's paper at Geneva – but surely you must have realised that from the context?') You can also play on this disingenuous line if they persistently block requests for facts: '... sorry you could not tell me the figures from 1999-2001, but it does not matter as I have now found them in the 2002 report. Your answer shows that you cannot have read the report, which indeed is obvious from some of the false assumptions in the introduction to the plan...'

Inconsistency: 'This is not the reason that Councillor Forthright gave at the original meeting in the town hall.' 'This is in conflict with ministry circular 113/67.' 'You did not enforce this in 2004 in an identical instance.' Do not, of course, state what the circular or the councillor said – let them sweat.

Inefficiency: '... when your representative arrived it transpired that no one had told her the subject of the meeting ...'; '... now appears that you were in the building all the time, while we were being sent away because you ...'; '... since you appear to have lost the minutes, I enclose a copy.'

Favouritism, especially of influential people. '… cannot of course expect the privileges you extend to Sir William by asking you to visit us instead of our awaiting your pleasure …'; '… quite understand that property as expensive as that in The Grove must receive special attention from your staff; nevertheless we too pay council tax, even if not in the same band…'; '… now find from Lady Cartridge that all her letters have been answered by return of post, while mine have taken between nine and 22 days…'

Trespassing on politicians' territory. '… policy you speak of is certainly not the council's – this was made clear at Thursday's council meeting with Councillor Brick. If the staff in the Planning Office have decided amongst themselves how the borough shall be developed, when may we expect the electors to be informed?'

Trespassing on other departments' territory. This can be encouraged by judicious timing: '… glad to know that arrangements are being made for schooling to continue during stage 11. Perhaps you could inform the Education Department of this, since their letter of the same date as yours says "no discussions have taken place as yet' ". It can also be helpful to your cause to circulate copies of your emails and letters: '… very happy to accept your explanation on the telephone this morning that it was the ministry and not you who had slipped up …' (copy to ministry).

Bureaucratic arrogance. '… of course appreciate (and perhaps you will permit me to add that your manner on the telephone makes it clear) that you are a busy and important person, and ordinary members of the public are a nuisance. But do please realise that our homes, even if they are much less imposing than yours in The Avenue, matter desperately to us...'

CASE STUDY: Appledoor quary protest

At the first hearing the applicant claimed that this case had important national implications, which would have immensely serious repercussions if his application was rejected. So the Action Committee replied that if that were so, the application should be called in by the Deputy Prime Minister and decided in Whitehall rather than Somerset. They wrote to his office and received a reply that it was only a local issue, which demolished the applicant's claim.

It is frequently a good technique to keep a shot in your locker. Your initial letter or email on any topic will draw their fire, but it will also unmask their batteries. So keep back one important fact for your second letter or email: '... in reply to your point that I should have ascertained the details from the Borough Surveyors' office, that is precisely what I tried to do. I called there on May 13th, and was told by Mrs Clam that the facts were not to be made available to the general public.'

One of the standard bureaucratic responses is simply not to reply unless prodded, or to delay replying for a long time to gain breathing space, rather like lobbing in lawn tennis. You therefore have to stand at the net for the epistolary equivalent of a drop-shot, something that makes them move like lighting in order to save the point. To achieve this it is important to conduct your correspondence with the top person, even though their subordinates are replying on their behalf. There is a special reason for this: if you score a valuable point in correspondence with a subordinate official, the top person can always say, 'Your case has only just been brought to my notice. I am sorry about the confusion – there seems to have been a slip up somewhere.' (Public officials sell their subordinates down the river more readily than any but the very largest business corporations.) They cannot say this if the reply will be, 'I am surprised the case has only just been brought to your notice, since it was to you I addressed the letter.' – and their subordinate will treat your letter that much more carefully for knowing that the reply carries their boss's reputation as well as their own.

You can also prod procrastinating bureaucrats by invoking an authority from a higher level. When dealing with the town hall a letter to the minister responsible for local government simply listing the delays (there need to be two or three at least of 10 days to a fortnight) will elicit a neutral reply: '… sorry for the delay, but must ask you to be patient since our local government officers are understaffed and overworked …' The correspondence will nevertheless be sent down to the department, and it is a law of correspondence as of gravity that the greater the height from which it descends, the greater the force with which it hits the target. They will not want another such letter in a month's time.

Another ploy is to write to Buckingham Palace. The Queen's staff cannot of course do more than pass your letter on to the relevant office, but the fact of its having come from the Palace gives it a certain magical quality which should ensure swifter replies in the future. There is scarcely a public official in this country over the age of 40 whose mind does not from time to time revolve around the possibility of an appearance in an Honours List, and what is more they know very little about how the system operates in practice. Will their name be entered in the Royal Black Book if there are three complaints about their actions within 12 months? Will a frown darken the royal brow when the name of the Deputy Chief Planning Officer for North Wessex crops up over cocktails at Sandringham? It may be wildly unlikely, but then a couple of lines on the map changing the route of the pylons is a small premium if it will insure them against such an awful possibility.

Babies
for Beginners
Roni Jay

"A perfect first book for all new mums and dads confused by parenthood." *Pregnancy*

At last, here is the book for every new parent who's never been quite sure what a cradle cap is and whether you need one. *Babies for Beginners* cuts away the crap – the unnecessary equipment, the overfussy advice – and gives you the absolute basics of babycare: keep the baby alive, at all costs, and try to stop it getting too hungry.

From bedtime to bathtime, mealtime to playtime, this book highlights the core *objective* of each exercise (for example, get the baby bathed) and the *key focus* (don't drown it). By exploding the myths around each aspect of babycare, the book explains what is necessary and what is a bonus; what equipment is essential and what you can do without.

Babies for Beginners is the perfect book for every first time mother who's confused by all the advice and can't believe it's really necessary to spend that much money. And it's the ultimate guide for every father looking for an excuse to get out of ante-natal classes.

Roni Jay is a professional author whose books include *KIDS & Co: winning business tactics for every family*. She is the mother of three young children, and stepmother to three grown up ones.

This edition contains new material

£7.99

Tidy Your Room

Getting your kids to do the things they hate

Are you sick of yelling at the kids to hang up their clothes? Tired of telling them to do their homework? Fed up nagging them to put their plate in the dishwasher? You're not the only one. Here, at last, is a practical guide to help you motivate them and get them on your side.

Parenting journalist Jane Bidder draws on the advice of many other parents as well as her own experience as a mother of three, to bring you this invaluable guide to getting your kids to do the things they hate.

The book includes:
- what chores are suitable at what age, and how to get them to co-operate
- getting homework done without stress
- where pocket money fits into the equation

Tidy Your Room is the book for any parent with a child from toddlerhood through to leaving home, and anyone who has ever had trouble getting their kids to do chores or homework. That's just about all of us, then.

Jane Bidder is a professional author and journalist who writes extensively for parents. She also writes fiction as Sophie King. She has three children, the eldest two of whom are now at university, so she has extensive personal as well as professional experience of getting kids to do the things they hate. She is the author of *What Every Parent Should Know Before Their Child Goes to University*.

Price £7.99

The GARDENER'S POCKET BIBLE

EVERY GARDENING RULE OF THUMB
at your fingertips

Do you know every gardening technique and rule of thumb off pat? Or do you occasionally straighten up from your digging to try and remember exactly what you're meant to be doing? How deep should you plant these bulbs? Was it now you were supposed to prune this rose, or in February? Can you compost this weed? Is it OK to plant out these seedlings now?

It's such a pain having to go indoors, kick off your boots, shed your outdoor clothes and start looking up the answer to your question in some great gardening tome. And that's where *The Gardener's Pocket Bible* comes in. Because now, you can stay in the garden and look up all those essential facts and figures in an instant. At your fingertips you'll have all the answers to your on-the-spot questions such as:

- Which plants do you need to protect from frost?
- When should you cut the hedge?
- What plants need staking, and when?
- How can you get rid of greenfly without using pesticides?

This indispensible little guide will tell you what you need to know, when you need to know it – and will save you thumbing through gardening encyclopedias when what you actually want to do is get on with the gardening.

£7.99